Douglas Livingstone

SELECTED POEMS

AD. DONKER/PUBLISHER

AD. DONKER (PTY) LTD
A subsidiary of Donker Holdings (Pty) Ltd
P O Box 41021
Craighall
2024

This selection first published 1984
Reprinted 1987

ISBN 0 86852 041 1 (hardback)
ISBN 0 86852 042 X (paperback)

Typeset by Triangle Typesetters (Pty) Ltd, Johannesburg
Printed and bound by National Book Printers,
Goodwood, Cape

CONTENTS

ACKNOWLEDGEMENTS AND SOURCES

Part 1 is a selection from *The Skull in the Mud* (Dulwich: Outposts Publications, 1960).

Part 2 is a selection from *The Sea My Winding Sheet,* a verse play first broadcast by the Rhodesian (Federal) Broadcasting Corporation in 1963 directed by John Parry; first staged (accompanied by a printed version) by the Theatre Workshop Company (Durban, 1971) directed by Pieter Scholtz; the whole script included in *Theatre One* edited by Stephen Gray (Johannesburg: Ad. Donker, 1978).

Part 3 is a selection from *Sjambok and Other Poems from Africa* (London: Oxford University Press, 1964).

Part 4 includes a selection of Shona poems translated with Phillippa Berlyn from '8 Shona Poems' (*The London Magazine,* January 1968) originals by Wilson Chivaura, Noel Kashaya, Joseph Kumbirai, Gibson Mandishona, Edgar Musarira, Solomon Mutswairo and Henry Pote; the Hungarian poem is by Gyula Illyés, translated with Thomas Kabdebo, and appeared in *A Tribute to Gyula Illyés* edited by Thomas Kabdebo and Paul Tabori (Washington: The Occidental Press, 1968); my translation of the French poem by José-Maria de Hérédia first appeared in *A Rosary of Bone,* second enlarged edition (Cape Town: David Philip, 1983).

Part 5 is a poem from my section of *Poems*, with Thomas Kinsella and Anne Sexton (London: OUP, 1968).

Part 6 is a selection from *Eyes Closed Against the Sun* (London: OUP, 1970).

Part 7 is a selection from *A Rosary of Bone* (Cape Town: David Philip, 1975, and the enlarged edition of 1983).

Part 8 is a selection of Giovanni Jacopo's meditations which first appeared in *Bolt* (March 1971), *Seer* (no. 1, 1972), *Ophir* (no. 23, 1976), *The Bloody Horse* (nos. 1 and 2, 1980) and *The London Magazine* (March 1982).

9

Part 9 is a selection from *The Anvil's Undertone* (Johannesburg: Ad. Donker, 1978).

Part 10 includes a poem from *Olive Schreiner and After* edited by Malvern van Wyk Smith and Don Maclennan (Cape Town: David Philip, 1983); and a poem quoted by Tony Morphet in *Reality* (May 1983).

Part 11 is Giovanni Jacopo's meditation included in *Momentum: On Recent South African Writing* edited by M.J. Daymond, J.U. Jacobs and Margaret Lenta (Pietermaritzburg: Natal University Press, 1984).

Minor emendations have been made to a few of the early poems.

I from

THE SKULL IN THE MUD
1960

Africa

Red dawn; the clang of hammer suns; winged night.
The ruby freshness furnaced. Then the kite
of evening swarms the air to cool the hush.
The night's black mouth split-stretches for the bite

that gulps the land, swift-spitting stars like crumbs.
Again, the dawn spreads eager blood-stained thumbs
to start the avalanching anvil-rush
of gongs. The sun erupts and, stunning, numbs

the drawn pale eyelid. Frail-legged herons walk:
black, white and brown; fitful or swift, they stalk
their daily crust on farm and mine; while plush
executive newts telephone and talk.

A sanguine Earth bowls languid through the lakes
of Einstein's fields of linear mistakes,
and Africa spreads sideways to the crush.
Upon an antheap, parched, a buck awakes.

The Skull in the Mud

Braced by the aqualung, and hot
help-handed by two small black boys,
the dam-site twisting, stamped with noise,
his harness like some cloth garrotte,

he sank suddenly weightless down
into the rusty box of death —
seventy feet in one slow breath —
enmeshed within the spiked steel gown

of sheet-piling, barbed, hawsered gloom;
stiff pipes rigging the jagged saw-
toothed web of metal, clutch and claw
snarled about the coffin-shaped room.

He nudged the bottom, tripped the light,
saw not nine inches from his nose
a yellow skull, dull, tenebrose,
jawless on muds of liquid night.

Vomited up from swarthy rocks
lining the river's ancient bed,
it perched, sardonic, gently dead,
tossed up by new construction shocks.

The pair exchanged a filmy stare
in cooling silence in the mud,
tried to plumb through the river's blood
their alienness, groped for the rare

meaning in this contact of race,
striving to bridge the yawn of years,
of centuries, of Man-old fears:
unlooked for ending, face to face.

14

Each now at one with this the last
levelling constituency —
thalamic, wordless fluency —
they formed, de-formed and drowned their past.

Politely he backed, broke the tie.
The skull's wink flicked swift as a knife:
a small minnow intent on life
shot twinkling from one hollow eye.

(Kariba, 1957)

The Unknown Refugee

The hands are curled and numb. The opaque eyes
are shutters drawn on sun, on naked soul.
Dim, secret, silent, brother to the mole,
he slumps beneath his corrugated skies.
His form is prone and frail. The slackened thighs
splay limply on old empty sacks of coal
while each sole flaunts its draughty abject hole.
The grate sighs damply, steaming last week's lies.
Horizons pitch, are lost. These went before:
my wife, my skills. Gone all of me that can
reorientate my sovereign state of War,
of dehabilitates, the also-ran.
Acceptance. This is all I crave. No more.
For I am also brother to the Man.

Drought

The drumming on the dusty, dry-walled ear,
the slime on aching, parch-caked, crackling lip,
the dusty doorway's drooping, mote-filled dip
all semaphore an atavistic fear.
This crooked pain, twisted archaic spear
bent, hurled and splintered by the fruitless flip
against the mastodon's great leathered hip
means 'Will it ever rain again? This year?'
The rangy, racial leopard easy lopes
the yellow veld before the leaping rains.
Then men in hollow doorways nail their hopes
upon the slaking of the thirsty plains;
and who knifes who and who will stretch the ropes
dissolves in clean-swept, swirling, swollen drains.

To Our Tomorrows

When you and I are far too old to care
these viruses will be mutating still.
Dictators with their boring speeches will
be spitting out their ancient saltless fare
— or Thirty-third Reich snarling from its lair.
And yet this flaunting rose shall always fill
our nostrils with its scent, that rainbird thrill
our hardening eardrums with its liquid air.
The tide of evil starts its flow with Man;
and though the lethal mushroom bells now ring
sly knells of doom, the silent seeds will span
the bridge of life as far as ages fling.
Fear, as only our foolish fancies can,
that flood of evil: when the roses sing.

Night Club Pianist

A loose-limbed sloucher with a butt on his lip,
a lack-a-daisy tinkle and a feather-fingered flip,
three dreg-bottomed glasses on the instrument's stained
                                                    top,
a weary dreary number that never seems to stop;
a rumbled syncopation that quickly, smoothly, dies,
a smoky hushed dim atmosphere, lethargic hips and eyes,
a slow hypnotic rhythm with a metronomic slur,
unsudden soothing discords that rumble, fade and purr;
the tables slowly empty, the waiters drift away,
alone and lonely, fingering, he welcomes in the day.

Amphoræ

The yellow beach road writhes its sandy skin
under an arch between the white-washed walls
to the bay where a small brown fishing boat,
lateen-rigged, daubs the blue. With gallantry
the stone arch helps the creepers cross the road.
Open windows hint sultry mysteries —
exciting scents of Aphrodite's hair,
sweet, dusky, warming muliebrity —
with perhaps the dark tints of sandalwood.

On a doorstep, two amphoræ, beaded,
slim and black, and obviously wine-cool,
strike an uneven, still, sharp, watchful pose.

If you half close your eyes, pulling low
fringed lashes, the man on the down-turned tub,
idly whittling, becomes a valued friend
full of wise and mocking terseness. Trojan,
completely old-Levantic, is his air.

Squinting against the white sun, you can walk,
chequered by shade and shine, down the beach road,
past the houses and the phocine wine jars
and muffled women's whispers from the rooms.
Down — scuffing down — past bollards to the bay.
There, quite alone, enter the dancing, blue
wrinkled waters, and, making of yourself
a libation, merge wetly with the sea.

Swaying, sea-drunkenly on light toe-tips,
dream-striding between the ferny seaweed
and shards of old amphoræ, where the winds
cast them, filled once with dates or smoky oils;
down — where the water furls, low, cool and green,
by silently waiting, weightless and deep,

you can meet — arrived with a percheron's
suddenness — a dolphin, smile-snouted, gay,
and very Latin, making strong the wish
to stay submerged in all this palpable sea:
an atavistic hearkening to live
inhaling these slow waters thick with life
you have exchanged for insubstantial air.

Departure

Gleaming backs cloak the dirty deck
with cargo. The new franchise, the old trip
weight puffily each obsidian eye.
Lizard-like they hear the foreman's bawl and beck

knitting whoop and wharf of the docks.
Skull-white and skeletal the ghostly ship
flicks oily cables snakily awry.
Foam slowly churns in smoky swirls to lap the rocks

crouched at the harbour mouth. Light jumps
from off the wavelets. The small, tin twin cranes
stick angle-poised against the sky-high blue.
Self-consciously, with coughings, rhythmic, muffled
                                    thumps,

the ship swims, lurching, fast away.
Disturbed, the sun regrips the greasy brains
of watchers, melts their moulting bones to glue,
speeds the lumpy vessels in their slide back to clay.

The port, its daily duty done,
relaxes, slumps in languid torpor, bakes
somnolently. The porters grope for shade,
blindly grasping, with dull curses, swat at the sun.

The solid air boils on the winch.
The sheet-ironed capital of all the lakes
waits for the clanging smithy-heat to fade,
pulls on fly-blown, mephitic shroudings inch by inch.

2 from

THE SEA MY WINDING SHEET
1963, 1971, 1978

(The play retells the myth — in 'classical' and contemporary speech modes and rhythms — of the 24 Titans who burst volcanically from the earth's crust and assailed Olympus, haven of the gods. The largest and gentlest of the giants was Adamastor. He was diverted by the sea goddess Thetis with whom he fell in love. The gods called on Herakles, a mortal, for help who responded by clubbing down all the Titans. The dying giants all petrified into the various continents, land-masses and the larger islands. Doris, mother of Thetis, describes the event: 'Herakles counting corpses, near forgot, But searching, found and pulped the Giant's head As he lay dying, half-submerged by tides. This Giant, born with travail for his lot, Divided, doomed, was in confusion led. Around his shores my lovely Thetis rides. With thorn and grassy plain his form is draped. The continent of Africa is shaped.' Some believe Adamastor is not quite dead yet, but suffered some alteration of personality and temper from the experience.)

'In Corridors and Labyrinths My Mind'

The Genius of Earth:
   In corridors and labyrinths my mind
   Wends damply haunted to a misted deep
   Where lurks mad-ego pacing without sleep
   On wet and echoing streets thin-walled and vined
   With veins, a stagnant tombstone yet unsigned.
   Down here my vestige soul has built its keep
   To fortify from forms that subtly creep
   Well-hidden from the fearful glance behind.
   I feel and hear a deep evoking Call.
   Now phantoms chase me from my tunnelled pit:
   Bats scream and snakes with avid moilings crawl
   Upon their quarry. Hopeless, lost, I flit
   To slump exhausted near my skull's last wall
   While demons rush through, over, out of it.

'The Empty Villa Stands'

Adamastor:

The empty villa stands back for the road,
Sad-faced behind cypresses like a bloodhound,
Its nose on the paws of the drive, asleep.
    A hermetic door folded back
    For your touch and you entered
    Gentle-eyed, entranced.

The villa locks an arm on a courtyard
Of still palm-trees; where a stone dolphin leaps
From the vague square of a playing-card pool,
    Where oxygen-blue hyacinths
    Depict a thirteen of hearts.
    Then you found the tap.

The fountain made a crystal chandelier
Tinkle silver shards in the evening air.
Nothing else moved except you moving air
    As you looked into one dark-
    Panelled room after another,
    Through their mirror-panes.

The howdah of a made, canopied bed
Attracted you a while before you left it,
Drifting speculatively, one bare foot
    Before the other. Then, I suppose,
    You danced around the fountain,
    Weeping, half the night.

I found you just before the dawn, face down
And drenched among the silent lily-pads.
The stone flags, the vertebraed trees can hold,
    Contained within themselves, the sun's
    Nourishment only until near
    Midnight in that place.

'A Pleated Apron of Wrinkled Sand'

Thetis:

A pleated apron of wrinkled sand
Nursed by two wide, hard and rusting forearms
Flung out at the pliant smoke-screening surf,
Buried in the blue mother's belly who
Flinches, evades, twists, returns to smother
With her suckling and desperate breathing.

Alone, alone, he sleeps there fitfully.
Overhead, Apollo, the polished gong
Pulses brazen notes, sings on fiery beams,
Streaming his burning comet-banner through
The bubble of day; drowning; his furnace
Wastes in the sky-pools every evening.

A coolly crop-haired and orange lichen
Swims over these iron-muscled rock-veins.
Down here was hoisted to the tangy winds
A naked, real and first momentous love
Which was whipped to tattered memory's shreds,
Blown, defenceless to where all sunsets die.

The freedom of seas on ribs of children
Cools the loin-scouring sands of innocence.
Now, deep in his heartland creaks the grind of
Shifting metal sinews. Asleep he drives,
With sad, shaking, shuddering, hopeless thuds,
Those great worn, knotted fists into the sea.

Once I raised up a man from the sea.
And now I have pulled down a man to the sea.

'I Do Not Know What Makes Me Love the Night'

Thetis:
    I do not know what makes me love the night
    In which you walk so sadly and alone,
    Aloof and silent, filmy in the light
    Glared from a moon whose face frowns ice and stone.
    I do not know what makes me fear the trees
    That sentry down the path you move along;
    Black scudding clouds; lost echoes of far seas;
    The solitude within a night-bird's song.
    I think this is the country of the dead:
    Here, fear is joined to love in agony.
    Too distant from my call to turn your head,
    I see you drifting slow away from me
    To lands of precognition I'd forsake
    To find that stealthy dawn, and us, awake.

'When Once We Walked'

Adamastor:
    When once we walked, my hand in lilting hand,
    Upon that silky, mooning, distant shore,
    The night surrounded all that lay before
    Save glinting dunes, a skyline to the strand.
    And as we walked, eyes on that promised land
    We swore we could not love each other more,
    That darkness was a Time-preceding door
    Which opened on a place of warmer sand.
    Now I have bled my giant's heart of love,
    And burst my skull; an ocean's storming reach
    My gain, and in my hand a seaweed glove,
    Soiled by the years — an emptiness to teach
    This sorrow from the darkling sky above:
    The death of all such children of the beach.

'New Men Will Clump About'

Narrator:
New men will clump about and raise the dust,
Swing a stiffly articulated hip
To bridge small fissures scored into her crust,
While mutters pass from lip to crater-lip.

The tractors and prefabs will scar her seas
With tracks and alloys; diamond-booted drills
Inject and measure her by tall degrees.
Her temperature, soaring upon the hills

As sunlight blindly edges on her face,
Will shepherd them, melting, to the cold cubes
Prepared below the needle peaks that lace
The songs of constant stars in shortwave tubes.

On earth, one hopes, lovers will watch this light
The sun still hangs for them each cloudless night.

'When That Tough Olympian Thug'

Narrator:
When that tough Olympian thug found him and pulped
                                                    his head
he fell on parted seas and slept for centuries.
The thorns and antheaps, embalming him for dead,
    sent foetal dreams of earth's wet glaucous yolk
    until a short in Space or Time was reached that spoke.

Crackling flecks occultly stung his continental stones
with shocks from out the void. The pumping tocsin
                                                    chimed.
Bright gold corpuscles sped to his oily bones.
    In his dimmed soul the early a.m. spark
    was fought, rebuffed; curled and repelled the dark.

A few blades of scrub quivered. The girls on dolphins
                                                    steered
about his sandy fringe, hymning his antennae
with ancient shortwave taunts. Leading them all reared
    the mother of Achilles, laughing; back
    to stretch again this lover on her rack.

Memories of an atomic club dotting him one,
wrenched to be whirled from some pre-Nordic
                                                    Yggdrasil—
if Time's a .38 repeater — he was done:
    no rifling of his guts by knives impure,
    self-consumption would be slower and more sure.

In the evening we sit quietly as the fireflies pass,
contemplating the icecubes or the embered day,
teeth tapping lightly on the sundowning glass,
    hailing the woman, the tree and the beast,
    and salivate in foretaste of the feast.

3 from
SJAMBOK *and Other Poems from Africa*
1964

Lake Morning in Autumn

Before sunrise the stork was there
resting the pillow of his body
on stick legs growing from the water.

A flickering gust of pencil-slanted rain
swept over the chill autumn morning;
and he, too tired to arrange

his wind-buffeted plumage,
perched swaying a little,
neck flattened, ruminative,

beak on chest, contemplative eye
filmy with star vistas and hollow
black migratory leagues, strangely,

ponderously alone and some weeks
early. The dawn struck and everything,
sky, water, bird, reeds

was blood and gold. He sighed.
Stretching his wings he clubbed
the air; slowly, regally, so very tired,

aiming his beak he carefully climbed
inclining to his invisible tunnel of sky,
his feet trailing a long, long time.

The King

Old Tawny's mane is moth-
eaten now, a balding monk's tonsure,
and his fluid thigh muscles flop
slack as an exhausted boxer's;

Creaks a little and is
just a fraction under fast (he's lame)
in those last short lethal rushes
at the slim white-eyed winging game;

Can catch them still of course,
the horny old claws combing crimson
from the velvet flanks in long scores,
here in the game-park's environs;

Each year, panting heavily,
manages with aged urbanity
to smile full-faced and yellowly
at a thousand box cameras.

Leviathan

A puff-adder, khaki,
fatter than a stocking of pus
except for its short thin tail,
obese and quick
as certain light footed dancers
took a dozing lizard.

Scaly little monster
with delicate hands and feet
stupidly sluggish in the sun.
Panting, true,
but lizards breathe mostly
as if their lives depended.

Gone.
Enveloped by a slack
wormy yellow bowel.

O Jonah, to tumble to
those sickly deadly depths,
slick walled, implacably black.

Vulture

On ragged black sails
he soars hovering over
everything and death;
a blight in the eye
of the stunning sun.

An acquisitive droop
of beak, head and neck
dangles, dully angling,
a sentient pendulum
next to his keeled chest.

His eyes peer, piously
bloodless and hooded,
far-sighted, blighting
grasses, trees, hill-passes,
stones, streams, bones, bleached bones

with the tacky rags
of flesh adherent.
A slow ritual fold
of candid devil's palms
in blasphemous prayer—

the still wings sweep closed—
the hyena of skies
plummets from the pulpit
of a tall boredom,
swallowing as he falls.

He brakes lazily
before his back breaks
to settle on two
creaky final wing-beats
flinging twin dust-winds.

He squats once fearfully.
Flushed with unhealthy plush
and pregustatory
satisfaction, head back,
he jumps lumpishly up.

Slack neck with the pecked
skin thinly shaking, he
sidles aside, then stumps
his deliberate banker's
gait to the stinking meal.

Sax and Marimbas

Coals frowning in the half-sawn petrol drum
flick sparks from the darkness of intent eyes,
an angry orange sheen from the glared teeth,
under a starpocked April-cloudless sky.

But not the saxman, shadowy, slit-eyed,
mouth melting into reed, his shirtless bent
body hanging a dim question mark or
gallows to his luminous instrument.

The two marimba players squat drumming,
sweating grandly; robustly mallet-spilled,
the cracked machine-gun notes are scattering,
round, xylophonic and unscalable.

And over all that crouching motionless
watchful land webs an incandescence
of wailed skeins, stitching skulls, threading diaphragms:
new blues for harsh and ancient innocence.

Pteranodon

A seven year old herd boy,
ragged happy and vacant,
sits alone playing the stonegame,
his back to the five
thin healthy head grazing.

Across the valley
the distant warts of huts
squat on the wrist of the hill.

Long believed extinct,
there was no one
but the walleyed
stampeding clot of cattle
to see the two dozen
feet of dusty leather
wingspread, hear the wet
crush of long toothed jaws closing,
the snap of vertebrae,
and nothing, nothing at all
the flight away
with the broken rabbit boy
one limb slow waving.

Dark Caesar's Child

You are the thirty-third this month,
    flesh of the swelling mother-fruit.
Your swollen mouth

is silent. Strapped polythene veins
    swoop blood to your mother's dry shell,
the sap-filled vines

pricked into black ankle and wrist.
    Quickly, precise, the needles shoot
swiftly to wrest

the bruised gash closed. The cloaking gauze
    breathes tremulously in the smell
of magicked gas

lingering in the starched white room.
    Your mother is fine, little man,
so why so glum?

Perhaps because the room is up-
    side down and white faces dream new.
Strain, strive to cap

this achievement of birth and *live.*
    There are more spells but, *start your span,
become alive.*

Your raisin face wrinkles with fear.
    The cave is closed. Breathing in, you
attack the air.

The Visionary

A witch doctor treated him for trachoma
funnelling the dry powdered root,
more caustic than mustard gas,
into each brown, red-haloed pupil.

The lances ran through to rest
on the back of his skull for a few weeks
after he had stumbled, numb, speechless,
groping even the ground with hands
individually terrified of scorpions, home.

For two years he sat in the doorway
while his wives ministered beer
mealie-meal, sometimes meat,
avoiding in a half circle his blind stare.

One night he followed something alone,
spouses and progeny snoring unaware,
not bothering to wake the small child
that led him tetherlike on a stick,
fell into a dry well and died upside down.

She-Jackal

As the sun fell west he composed himself
against a pinetree bole, happily smooth
a yard above the soft sprung-needle ground
and punched open one of his two beercans.

The hillside sloped sharply and as he lay
propped, sipping and watching the purple hills
with their horizon-long yellowred banners
silently snapping and cracking on crests,
all convex and magnified, almost still,
the other side of the deep shadowed valley,
he saw a shamelessly feminine curved
Africa—usually so male and wrinkled—
blatant under the first opened stars.

Evilly panting and smiling, a jackal
stood near: razor ribs, warty shrivelled dugs,
hourglass loins and lean wire legs quivering;
the plump feeding ticks studding her bare flanks.
They looked at each other, obviously
disliking what they saw, both warily
tensed, although she retained her polished smile;
he, measuring jumps from her and his stick.

So, you mangy chewer of carrion,
he thought it directly and impolitely,
camp follower of filthy offal-thieves,
what the hell are you drooling over, bitch?
this meat is alive with a nearly full
tin of chemical malt in its right hand.

She made no reply so he flung it hard
and inaccurately and she was gone
apparently without moving; the tin
fanned arcs of liquid silver an instant
of flight against the exhausted sunset.

He got up stiffly and climbed higher, pillared
on the one hand by his staff of bamboo;
in the other, his remaining beercan.
From up there, there might be some sunset left.

Return Valves

From where the exhaustless landrover stood expired
    dragged there by the last of its tired, abused
    and bonneted horses, pulseless and juiceless,
To the farmhouse was three wood-iron moonless miles—
    a crisp walk through the cold and battened dark
    under shivering tarred planks holed for stars.

I found myself a nigger in a blackbirder's
    hold, rocking, chained, raftered and held by these
    leaky endless tunnels of cypresses:
Eyes rolling; seasick; reeling; speeding ahead of
    the scurvy; unknown America not
    invented; bloody from an Arab's goad.

Freed and tumbled up to the good old U.S.A.
    I flexed and scowled in the freetraders' mart.
    In time my white corpuscles eddied past,
Rootless and about, like soft cotton-bolls in J.
    Brown's body, his red-blood notes ricochetting
    as the genes fled before each mouldering.

I, carcinoma-grown, unaired and mushroomy,
    my hating heart slow snaking in its fuse,
    nun-eyed, a bird, embraced the telling blues.
An old yellow river, flaccid, with crummy
    conical huts and muddy yam patches
    waterfalled and left a new rock of ages.

One hundred yards from the stolidly thatched farmhouse
    was when the coiled reef struck—I think it was
    the radiogram; certainly it is
Of no importance who activated that loud
    avenue-channelled smash of sound, that rich
    probing of lava, molten and volcanic.

Miles Davis behind the band-saw of his trumpet
    burring the darkwood ship of night to shreds
    with art, melody, genius even, yes,
But also with a tight wryly controlled triumph;
    Miles Davis with a brassy jazzhorn blur
    playing—destroying much—Bye Bye Blackbird.

All Africa listened to the shipwrecking waves
    of that Guernica of sound, the rigging-
    beetles stilled, the branching decks stopped creaking;
Only from the row of conical huts, humped graves
    behind the house, a tinny saucepan shed
    its tawdry counterpoint of Coke commercials.

Sunstrike

A solitary prospector
staggered, locked in a vision
of slate hills that capered
on the molten horizon.

Waterless, he came to where
a river had run, now a band
flowing only in ripples
of white unquenchable sand.

Cursing, he dug sporadically
here, here, as deep as his arm,
and sat quite still, eyes thirstily
incredulous on his palm.

A handful of alluvial
diamonds leered back, and more: mixed
in the scar, glinted globules
of rubies, emeralds, onyx.

And then he was swimming in fire
and drinking, splashing hot haloes
of glittering drops at the choir
of assembled carrion crows.

To a Dead Elephant

Old Python Nose with the wind-rolling ears:
   Hau! I remember it well when you came,
   thin, small, grey, twinkle-eyed, stumbling and lame,
to me, a lone boy with none of the fears
that stalked the elders. Friend, I had no tears
   for both our young losses; but all the same
   you robbed me of those sweet potatoes!
                            Fame
walked with us, both motherless, those coupled-years.

But who can tame the trumpeter, the hill
   who stands invisible with bright old eyes,
so slow, tree-bulky, dangerous and still?
   Why did you leave me to the elders' lies?
Both men, we meet again, but not my will
   wrought this antheap with flies and hamstrung thighs.

Stormshelter

Under the baobab tree, treaded
death, stroked in by the musty cats,
scratches silver on fleshy earth.
Threaded flame has unstitched and sundered
hollow thickets of bearded branches
blanched by a milk-wired ivy. Choleric
thunder staggers raging overhead.

'Never stand under trees in a storm.'
Old saws have an ancient rhythm
in them, but these dry, far from bold
norms and maxims are scalpel-severed
by the sharp, needle-thin lightning,
frightening reason behind the eye,
slivered into lank abstract forms.

Steel spears, slim, yielding and stained
lightly with water, rattle their points.
Jointed the hafts swing, tufted brightly,
maiming invisibly. The shafts reel
through the streaked Impi from Nowhere.
There is only one thing to do—
wheel, stamping, into that brittle rain.

Not This Once

I came upon a woman sitting
before the sea-wall on the beach
from behind; her singing,
facing the greasy grey wrestling reach

of storming waters, eyes closed
against the windy sand;
her voice flat pure and low,
altogether beautiful in some song

trite and popular, not much wryly
paid attention to its cadences; her
smoky hair streaked lightly
with a premature or artificial grey

blowing and lifting in streamers of notes;
slim she was, bony even her face
with a thin brown long throat
snaking from a commonplace dress,

but clean; tanned arms crossed
on her knees; so she sat singing
with wind and water, lost;
and being a bit of a romantic

sod at heart, loving women, the fire
in the race, perhaps overmuch,
I walked away controlling the desire
to intrude, protect, love, touch.

One Time

It seems a certain time ago: a-maybe
seven years or less, he
first took a woman underwater. In aqualungs
and bathing suits, hanging
in the pale liquid air
of a blue cathedral
—the sleeping pool of the limestone caves
to be precise—
face mask to mask,
wide-eyed and glass to glass,
they triumphed over the first knotty cotton fumblings
in the all embracing wetness.

Her hair, like a damp Medusa's,
flared upwards.

He remembers their delight at the silent
new experience,
their emulations of the passions
of dolphins
who are not after all
unhonourable
and very humorous
and humouring in their loveplay.

Then, he recalls his panic
when, with a mounting climax,
perhaps upside down, certainly weightless,
he had to cram her mouthpiece
back into her vacant lips, fishwide and cyanosed,
her eyes lightly closed,
and it was a long swim away
to the surface. (Her hair hung down on the journey.)

She did, of course, recover adequately
after a few splutters and with him gently
squeezing her ribs regularly
while finning desperately
upwards.
        But it was some time
before they tried it again
—some time after
and in shallower water.

As I Walk with Effrontery, Alone

As I walk with effrontery, alone,
by night, by day, through mists or lights or rain,
in parks and over fields, beneath the sky,
through traffic or in corridors of brick
I carry the scent of your body always
upon me and wear the same shirt until
I find it now stinks of me and has lost
its delicate swan-necked flagon of you.

As I walk with effrontery, alone,
among jostling labyrinths of grey hustlers
perhaps intent, who knows? who knows! upon
their own happy fornications, although
one could never guess it with certainty
from their glum stifled faces, I recall
our gay expertise and indecorum
on floors, on grass, on beds, the moonlit beach.

As I walk with effrontery, alone
and suddenly delighted at an apt
quick witticism of yours bursting like
the sun above a thunderous cliff of cloud,
wondering its mocking disrespectful rays
don't playfully illuminate a few
of the very sober pates about me,
I must quench an abrupt laugh with a cough.

As I walk with effrontery, alone,
I contemplate your murder to assuage
the carcinoma of my jealousy
thinking how next time I sprawl beside you,
a hot afternoon breeze probing the curtains,
my teeth against your honey coloured throat,
an instant's clench will salve it, slake it all—
the love, the fear, the channels of your life.

As I walk with effrontery, alone,
I know that I am lost and should be kept
incarcerated somewhere, peacefully
quiet and padded to recover from
this succubus that now inhabits me,
or whom I inhabit. And pray the gods
spare me that exorcism, electro-
convulsive or other fell therapy.

The Clocks

She was very old maintaining a daintiness
redolent of white lace and lavender-scented
toilet soap and with a certain prim kindness
to tradesmen and animals, ensconced as she thought
invulnerably in her jungle fortress
of potted plants and two clocks of copper and glass,
knick-knacks, bric-a-brac and antimacassars,
and on the wall a scimitar belonging to a dear
dead brother who was something in the Middle East.

On the piano which she never played now, lived
her cat, perched endlessly like a great brass Chinese
gong, immovable except for his slitted alien eyes
varying sometimes to the waning afternoon light.

Her abruptness with callers edged defensively
from under the shadows of her ignorance
and impatience for all things modern; but here
in this room where—her only idiosyncrasy:
the two clocks were never wound—time stood softly still,
her very proper heart warmed slightly to persons
presenting themselves discreetly as at a court.

She slept too long and late one silent morning,
a bible and a tract on moral instruction
geometrically centred and bare on the bedside
table, her sheets snowy and almost unwrinkled.

The great ginger tom eventually moved in
next-door to escape the fuss, where the neighbours were
kindly and the milk almost as regular.

An Evasion

An old man sits in wrinkled reverie.
A chiselling of violin music at dusk
evokes her, carving her composite husk
hewed from caryatids of his memory.

The blue smoke of the distant fir-clad hills
redolent of pine, marjoram and thyme
brings back her hair like strands of ancient rhyme
blowing over the weathered window sills.

Sometimes, the tired red cobras of her lips,
the crests of her teeth, widen, part at him
in false words. Her eyes mock over a rim
of glass, down-lashed, intent on secret sips.

His slim, suntanned dream moves light as moonlight
on water elusive to his slow grasp
as recalled from the time he rose to clasp
her shadowed form from out his shrunken night.

When she fades or will not come, his old dull
eyes film. He becomes aware of the snows
packed around the bottle of his heart and knows
the play of spidery fingers in his skull.

Her inconstancy at first delights and then
enrages him. In the end he forgives
everything. Dozing in the sun, he lives
for her alone; his own kin past his ken.

Another set of eyelids he could drop
behind these outward ones, like a bland shutter
or spades of death emptying earth upon her.
He does not choose to cause her life to stop.

from **Elements**

Fire

Did you hear, Quintus, what occurred
within their Temple forecourt yard
this morning?
          About the tenth hour
I think it was; the day bid fair
to seeming one of those without
my men and I being blackly cursed,
our greaves escape their aimed toad's spittle,
our ears unburned by rebels' tattle,
and but our staves needed to clear
a gruff-humoured path to the lair
in which they so jealously hoard
empty mysteries of their god.
I ordered my men to their ease
under the shade of the gateway's
funnelling walls. From there we saw
as good a fight, if I may say,
as Romans give: one man against
all those usurous black-garbed pests
that sit, couched like vultures and dogs,
rooking travellers for starving doves
and pouching quickly in their dress
good gold for paltry Temple dross.
(Four or five at each marble slab
they perch, importantly, and drub
coins on white stone and cash-hard palms!)

The clash of voices, clinks of realms
falling and the uproar—far worse
than any Syrian market-place—
all stopped at one great roared command.
A young man, a flail in his hand,
his muscles bunched—a carpenter,

56

I hear, from the interior—
charged at those heaped precious tables,
kicked away the wrought-iron trestles
of some and overturned the others.
Two priests ran up high-pitched as wethers
and screamed: 'Arrest him!' but I felt
I should wait and see if he would
be good metal for the Circus.

Released, the doves whirled above us.
Bawls echoed from the Temple-yard.
Stampeding like some Spanish herd
men ran from the place, followed through
by some few with broken legs, though
these, too, limped fast and merrily.
(Those slabs are thick and heavily
they must have crunched on the pious
feet of the faithful usurers!)

The rout was tickling but I kept
my stern Temple-Patrol face straight.
The man brushed past me afterwards.
I made no move for arrest.
I heard him shout it was *his* 'house';
perhaps it was. I liked his face.

Bamboo

One day in wet November where the thrash
   of thunders slit the glowering foundry sky
with molten saffron jags,

I wrung a bamboo root from rain-swamped death
   and fed her to a more maternal scar
scored higher on the earth.

She fanned her hidden lapping roots to sop
   the flood, uncoiled her snaky knotted grain
and toughly swelled with sap.

She spiked erect and spread her spears to add
   tall hornet-yellow, two-edged, dagger-green
straight whippily to God.

Now, baked and crackling clay holds her in vice;
   a sheen of silver cloaks the whispery
split organs of her voice.

A blunted sun stabs greedily from space:
   I squat within her shade and know a dry
and satisfactory peace.

4 TRANSLATIONS

Love
from the Shona of Wilson Chivaura

Love, my sister-in-law, has to be fried
like a mealie-cob in the pan of courtship,
sides reddening from the incessant turning
—the only love-philtre tempting to men.
Love, the seedling, must be cultivated
—all those choking weeds vigilantly pulled.
Love is a stomach, fainting or replete;
a roof, needing perpetual rethatching
to avoid its total replacement—patches
held ready for the inevitable holes.
Love needs constant honing, the well-used axe.
Hide love: it is not for hearthstone nor mortar,
or it gets defiled by dirt and ashes
like meat that has been breathed on by a crow.

Owl
from the Shona of Noel Kashaya

When the children are asleep, all light
extinguished, he starts to wheel
the world: this son-in-law of darkness.

With silent senses, his eyes *bambara*—
groundnuts in a hollow stone, he knows
everything he sees, despite the darkness.

At first light, the enemy emerging,
he hankers for his cave, remembering
every place he knows of friendly darkness.

Other birds begin with joy to weed
the hills as *their* Great Chief, the sun,
appears to rout, then banish, darkness.

Daylit songs of delight herald their greedy
open-beaked foragings; but Owl has pulled
the night about him, caved in darkness.

Dawn
from the Shona of Joseph Kumbirai

Cock-crow and early-rise!
Venus, the morning star, appears,
a first light, growing.

The sky is a blood-orange;
the first zestful breeze delights the heart
but shrivels up the morning star.

The roosters' voices fade
while the light gets brighter;
the elephants of dawn have finished washing.

The first dew steams
along with smoking hearths;
birds awaken, chirruping.

Brilliantly, pristine,
the great sun appears
like a large and glittering forehead.

Children warm their backs,
shouting: The sun,
the sun is King!

Their little polished heads
shimmer and glitter
like leaves turning from the west.

As the sun sets, so we set;
as the sun rises, so we rise:
the sun, the sun is King!

My Garden of Red Soil
from the Shona of Gibson Mandishona

A dove calling in the wild figtree by the cattle-kraal
awakens me early each day before the washing of the
                                    elephants of dawn,
and I consider happily, on getting up,
that a garden of red soil is better than all others.

Eagerly I run to it, the grass still wet with dew,
while an African waterhen cries in the still dark-shrouded
                                              forest.
My garden is big and the old ones say: It will be the death
                                           of him!
But when one is young and strong, hard work holds no
                                           fears.

A garden of red soil grows better than all others.
Just look at those nearby pumpkins ripening
—their long green tendrils trailing all over the place!
Arriving alone, you might think this a madman's garden—a
                          madman with green fingers.

The Little Beer Pot
from the Shona of Edgar Musarira

You're good as gold,
made from real earth
—earth that shines even when
uncooked—the rich earth.

Precious before you were moulded,
an egg in the hands of women,
baked in the fire's red embers,
your brown crimsoned with pride.

Drunkards are your friends:
lifting and patting you
they kiss your lips;
you're trusted because you're cool.

The Hills of Thirst
from the Shona of Solomon Mutswairo

How entrancing are the Hills of Thirst
which decorate the country of Chief Chiweshe!
How happy would I be if I could dream
myself back across the Sawi, near Gweshe.

How I admired those Hills of Thirst
plunging from their shadow with the sunrise;
or at sunset and with night drawing in,
I am back across the Rya—places that I love.

How bewitching is that Country of Thirst!
With the first rains, the trees flower.
The blossoms of the plain are white as ash
among the young green of *munhondo* trees, land of
                                    enticement.

How I would love to find myself at Chiweshe
listening to the new songs of the veld birds
and the songs from the comfortable villages
living in the past, living without care.

The Country of Thirst near the Sawi
is the country of rice, mealies and *rupoko*.
It is a land of flowing rivers
and the folk are filled with song.

Although I am far from the Land of Thirst,
being in a country which is like a desert,
how pleasant it is to recall it, dreaming
of being across from Gweshe, near the Sawi.

The Sun Goes Up and Up
from the Shona of Henry Pote

The sun goes up and up while you are at the drums,
consuming your strength at the skins
with undignified and unprofitable dancings
—while at home there is not even a chair.

The sun goes down and down, and you get drunk,
destroying your bowels, your brains, your manners
—while at home your children faint with hunger,
—while you, light-hearted, shout: We do what we like!

Night and day, month after year, you kill each other
—while your rivals swear oaths and prepare;
young men and women letting blood, or bleeding to death
—while old men and grandmothers, devouring granaries,
                                                    remain.

The sun goes up and up, and you complain
the clever ones among you use your strength, probing,
enriching themselves, succeeding, because you
care not about working for yourselves, helping each other,
                                                    peace.

You Cannot Escape
from the Hungarian of Gyula Illyés's 'Nem menekulhetsz'

We looked down into the ship's engine-room
where, among the pistons' steady beat
naked stokers scurried about
crimson as devils in the heat;
great gusts of boiling air escaped
the hatch as if from a door in hell—
What toil! I thought . . . but someone beside me
said: They're used to it, they know it well.

Sitting in a deckchair by the rail,
upon my lap a folded book,
blue mountains swam alongside, past me,
soothing my eyes, my tired look.
Hills and clouds of water — an unwritten
poem was all this, too — the slow
voyage — images woven in rhythms
to the muffled thumping below.

I swam over water, soared with the light,
happily knew I was beyond all now
high on the world's poetic stratum,
leaving below the unceasing row
of sweating and spitting and choking.
They're used to it, I told myself at last.
Or are they? And arrowing into me
came a cold sardonic shaft from the past.

Oh, are they? Did *you* ever get used to
(— you had a share in it —) that hoe?
Do you remember? Recall your father!
What did he get used to? Death's blow?
In the midst of fate and poverty
what man can get used to anything?

Agonized, I paced up and down
on a ship's deck, feeling its writhing.

You are a fool, I hissed at myself.
A traitor! just a traitor, nothing more,
amplified a voice within my heart,
while the thumping answered with metered echo:
Traitor! Liar! Miserable one!
Hireling, lying low! If once again
you found yourself among life's stokers
would you get used to the choking and pain?

I found myself against the rail
struggling, as if my father's fate
were cast beneath my feet, as if he stoked
again, day-labourer on the count's estate.
As if my father and all my ancestors
were toiling, panting, thumping down below
and crying upwards from the grave —
the deck made knuckle-raps against my sole.

Staring down at the water I saw
the blue landscape loping fast
away as if the motion weren't the ship's
but a thumping history rushing past.
As if it flung at me its ragings,
sickening me, its pitiless No
— spelling it out — you cannot forget,
you cannot escape, wherever you go.

A Presentiment of the Nile
from the French of José-Maria de Hérédia's 'Antoine et Cléopâtre'

The pair on the terrace looked down upon the scene:
All Egypt slept below the hot sky, stupefied;
The river rolled along its delta's black divide,
Past towns and hamlets, waters oily and unclean.

The Roman felt his heavy armour intervene
Between his triumphant heart and her yielding side.
She stirred in drowsy welcome — not to be denied
The voluptuous body of this childlike queen.

Her white face gleamed, framed by dark hair. The heady
                                          mist
Of her perfume inflamed him. Turning to be kissed,
She offered him her mouth; her pupils seemed alight.

The passionate Imperator, the strategist
Bent, seeing in those eyes gold flecks — with one new twist:
The vista of a sea where galleys broke in flight.

5 from
POEMS
1968

A Japanese Courtyard

White marble fountains
   snow drenched petals, glass fans grow
Lilies by moonlight.

Warm tears in water,
   frost of desolation: lost
Pearls in an ocean.

Cold porcelain tiles,
   night-chequered, caress two light,
Too hot, small bare feet.

Outside, night bustles
   assaulting shadowed cloisters,
Frustrated as seas.

Within, a still pool
   hides: tiger-toothed traffic rides
Skirting the lagoon.

6 from

EYES CLOSED AGAINST THE SUN

1970

A Flower for the Night

Where I lived for a childhood
the night grass was as magical as the moon;
coolly white and soft, like new snow beautiful,
and deeply piled by the monsoons.

There was a flower (I never learnt its name)
that bloomed one night a year,
following, with its delicate bluish face,
the arc that the full moon steered.

There was a garden of small temples,
a shrine to the wind and other deities,
where tea was served to guests in porcelain shells
carried over bridges of red-painted filigree.

On the low, carved tables scattered about
black pots stood etched with cloud-shaped trees;
each pot held a bud, each had its silent knot
from the waiting throng of, mostly, Chinese.

And then the moon rose fat-faced and yellow.
The few lanterns appeared to fade in the silver air.
In minutes, as in a spell, all the buds opened.
There were so many quiet people there.

The Explainer

I beg your pardon, Misha
Levenski, widow, without
children, of the used-violin

and sheet-music shop; cattle-trucked
to Treblinka; gassed, cremated
alone with a batch in '43.

I beg your pardon, you who
went up: violin-shaped smoke
while I was a boy in the sun;

whose immortal remains sometimes
I still breathe and, making me sneeze,
exclaim *Bless You!* Forgiveness I ask

for not shutting up after
knowledge, for not confining
myself to chimneys or to the

Cyclon B.   Incapable of
a talented silence: doing
my thing on birds and beasts of this earth

is to watch myself in case
I wake behind wire, holstered
with authority, jackboots on.

Vanderdecken

Sometimes alone at night
lying upon your surf-ski
far beyond the sharknet

drifting on the salt-wet belly
of your mistress the black ocean,
cool under a windless moonless sky

your dangling toes you hope
not luminous from below,
dozing to the sleepy remote

mutter of shorelusting breakers
you start hearing the thrash
of bone, foam and wake;

splintering yardage and thrumming
cords; creak, groan and rattle
of blocks—and, trembling

as you lie, wet from your own death-
salt, you hear the solitary
hopeless steady cursing in Dutch.

Aphrodite's Saturday Night

In the small chaotic bedroom above
his darkened shop, his scrambled shrine to love,
up there brightly lit and bedclothed tumbled
he awakes at fifty-three. His eyes stumbled
by importunate mirrors, five-foot-six;
in his naked complexion Europes mix;
belly swollen and grey, the hairy screws
of lank, lamp black are scratched; he gropes for shoes.

Dressed, buttonholed, he walks down to his shop
and threads the known and holy maze. A crop
of hunting prints are dangerously stacked
on black full-bosomed, generously cracked
and enormous chests bared to the dark.
A musty smell swells from the mounted lark,
blitheless in spirit. Glints glance off cabinets,
dressmakers' dummies, Georgian bassinets.

He weaves gently intent through walls of knives,
cutlasses, swords and kukris; Plutarch's *Lives;*
cold yellowing chessmen sullenly trapped
in ivory or ebony and the chapped
Queen Anne tea-sets and fire-cracked Chinese gongs;
brasses and lanterns; sets of chestnut tongs—
reaches and opens the door marked ƨƎUϘITИA
and stops for her in her street-lit patina.

She stands, six inches tall, inside the door,
listening to silence. This divine whore
is not the hacked, hackneyed one from Mylos,
but a softer, more slender and guileless
altogether one: head inclined, one hand
guarding the pubic from the public, and
fixed. He will not sell. Like all superior
courtesans, unpriced. He spurns every offer.

He bows. His moustache respectfully brushes
the top of her semiprecious head. Spruce as
a penguin, elated, key safe, he lets
himself out where the tunnelled night wind frets.
He wheels his stick as he walks, unafraid;
breathes, rinsing soggy lungs, uncreaks vertebrae.
He will march the park, ignore the lovers strewn
on every bench, watch for the errant moon.

Blue Stuff

Wall-to-wall city on a rainy night; eleven
stories up and the wonder-hour-hand when
is 4 a.m. with only a very quiet Kenton
accompanying the one-sky-lamp in

the corner. Yes, she's gone, warm to bed.
The floor feels strangely concrete-solid
despite the undermining gusts walled outside.
Wet beetles lie parked under street lamps, dead.

The wakeful rain musics back no April
in Paris; nor stale old Stars fell
on Alabama. Somewhere, space unfurls
its furnaced seasons. Somewhere, over the sill,

crooked as the iced-sucker wrapper flies,
the holiday surf, swelled into its own, says:
The sshun'sh gone. The night-tide ebbs and soughs
loud and lording it unchallenged upon the shores

of South Beach, North Beach, Country Club.
Even the sherry-drinkers have long stubbed
the last drag. The street's hands are cupped;
the stars, maybe forever, are all washed up.

Dive

Here, women wear the hawks' eyes
of old Egyptian friezes.
The old fruit at the bar limpwrists
his gin, shouting to beat the band:
'consenting adults' at Japanese
seamen who cannot understand
a word. A charged table overturns,
two barrel-shouldered managers
bulkily drift that way.

On the floor, young prostitutes
twist, maintain bouffants, look bored
with the hirsute arms of their whalers.
From its dais the band asserts for
all: it too has a Ticket to Ride
punched from behind a dozen wide-
open amplifiers. The fat whore
steps over the drunk on the steps:
'Call me bluebird', she says.

To a Chinese Lady
found on the beach in a dirty photograph

Your face so pretty but I wondered where,
picking you up,
jumped from somebody's jacket pocket
onto clean sand,
I had seen those eyes before.

Once, stopping next to a pink icing-sugar
English lady
in the Snake Park, middle-aged skirt too long,
who moved away
annoyed immediately, I saw a couple of
mambas doing it.
It was early Spring and they do it not
as some snakes do:
half-swallowing the other. The male lay
in gliding curls
along the female's back until
his upsidedown
belly met hers by twisting underneath
around, back over,
short tail lashing on her immobile one.
Indeed she was
immobile throughout, head off the ground,
almost queenly;
he thrashing about, knotting and squirming,
to flop his head
exhaustedly across her upcurved neck
(no love bites here!)
she staring, unmoving, at nothing—
black, alien eyes
holding nothing visible in focus.

So you stared with deep empty eyes at nothing,
body contorted

one presumes at the photographer's behest;
your partner holding
his head down out of sight on the far
side of your neck.
He appeared to be unashamed enough of
the rest of him:
one cannot recognize folk by their shanks;
and from this flank
he looked old, wrinkled in the space that had
distended for
few feasts in a lifetime of lean years.

As for the photographer, I suppose
he has to eat.
At least he is one of the causes we met.

Now you, girl, were lying on a good mat.
A pot plant stood
in one corner in one of those expensive
wood and brass tubs.
I think you may not own these. Probably
you were street-hired
with your stranger partner by the lensman
(:Madame – –,
I would like you to meet Mister–, please both
remove the clothes),
while beyond, you heard a shuffling avalanche
–the million feet
of your unconscious lovers. Or thought of lunch.

Down where your belly did not quite meet his,
I was able
to perceive with a certain wry interest
you were every bit
as other girls, not sideways-Chinese-style
–the weird canard

brought back with tea-chests in the flying ships
Thermopylae,
Taeping, Cutty Sark and *Ariel.*

I would like to know you . . . but this not in
a Biblical
sense of course!—Old Testaments frown such black
and testy thunders—
but know you as a very pretty girl
found in slightly
outré surrounds. Perhaps buy you a drink
and hear about
your philosophy. Learn of your childhood
spent darting under
the flapping bunting of the laundry-
woman's sampan
with a horde of small fierce brothers who were
Emperors among
the fishermen. That they now collectively
own an old junk
running refugees from the cryptic mainland.

I don't know what this poem is all about,
but madam 'tis
for thee and thee alone; and should it find you
it could be to say:
I'm pleased to meet you. I hope you are well
and are quite happy
in your work. But that your eyes in their absence
did disturb me,
but perhaps you were asked politely to do
the Inscrutable
East bit and that all is really well.
That by putting
you in the sea, this side, I intended
no disrespect;
that you are not quite as blind as I suspect.

Harbour

Claustrophobic,
                    oiled and
                                coiled cement
funnels footsteps along the embankment,
but there is
                    nobody
                                raincoated there:
no ship-on-shoes cleaves the fog-sheeted air
past tarpaulined
                    bare-poled
                                weekend sailors'
hulls and slipped signs of gone PEANUTS
                                BAIT sellers.
They stop:
                    nothing stops
                                to fling
signals at a silence that echoes nothing.
Catspaws anchor-
                    claw a wake
                                from the herewith
to the therefrom of a far-lighted berth.
Fog reshrouds
                    the clear: over
                                the water
a ghost-ship mourns darkly, and once more for
the vanished
                    day, the coming
                                separation,
to slide like night into a sloping ocean.
The steps
                    restart: plodding
                                prosaic, now
wading   invisible   encompassed   anyhow.

When

Running
like a redskin

arrowing
down blocks

tomahawking
through buffalo traffic

galloping barebacked
up flights

The quarry
Lasso of speech ready

no
it isn't

Pardon me madame
I thought

The march back
to Bosporus

stump-footing it
like a hoplite.

Steel Giraffes

There are, probably, somewhere
arms as petal-slight as hers;
there are probably somewhere
wrists as slim;
quite probably, someone has
hands as slender-leafed as hers;
the fingers, probably
bare of rings, as thin.

Certainly, there is nowhere
such a dolour
of funnels, mastings, yards,
filaments of dusk ringing shrouds
woven through the word goodbye,
riveted steel giraffes
tactfully looking elsewhere,
necks very still to the sky.

Fringes

Not a sparrow falls,
not even at the derelict dumping-site
on the outskirts of town.

A curlew calls
in sleep far up the river where night
slips off her dressing gown.

The mudflats hump
in the warm lagoon's disgorging jaws;
crying, the gulls sail in.

Dawn fans the sump
of civilization where the outlaws
shack up in shanties of tin.

Too early yet
for the shrimp-diggers, the quietening
of the all-night sea.

The sun, still wet,
pauses below its bunched brightening;
only the gulls have it free.

One Golgotha

The Kill

Jerked from meditation,
a tumult of hands dragged
me to a literary death.

I fought summary bestiality:
controlling the shades within,
stumbled to the crossroads.

One made prayer, one thudded
with a crucifix-haft;
I flinched from the water and garlic.

On their shoulders skulked
a terror of bloodied moons;
then the business of the mallet.

Lying in State

I await in this catafalque
fulfilment of the old lies
or a dolorous truth.

Two angels converse, rather
one: mercuric; the other
attentive, saturnine.

In my stiffenings and flakings
of leprous crackles,
I find room to consider.

The atrocity was performed
with a certain malignity:
I think my time will come.

Splinter of the True Cross

Splinter of the True Cross
I care not whence you hail.
Pale vehement researchers

in the glummer universities
have peered and proved you false,
but with polite divergencies

of theses and radio-
active-carbon datings.
One subtle group hold you,

by a certain corner-aspect,
a piece of saddlewood
carved for a camel's back;

another shoal of adepts knows,
hinged by that same corner, you held
a.Roman seadog's sea-chest closed.

Rust in this nail-hole has etched
haloes of salt-flavoured pith
where unwise theologians,

monks and sinners have probed
you with curious, sad or suppliant
tongues, tasting the centuries' blood.

Pitched and rolled in caravans,
rubbing the dingy hides raw
above trackless nights of sand,

or tossed in torpedo hulls
shuddering to oar-strokes
timed by the pitiless mallets—

for me, no great shakes
at research, you're good enough.
Your wood waxes to dim shapes

scaffolding the mystery
of camels, ships and men
swaying on their Calvaries.

The Heritage

I think of those unworldly men
beat out of hide, circumventive;
their galliass wives alien

across from the book between them.
Tramping plains and blue ravines: snake-
tracks down: up flanks: around wagon-

mining rocks: over parched aloes,
to the abuse of perched baboons.
Eternal hatreds, jealousies

born of each ford and decision;
brief alliances, long-term feuds
of cousin-cousin, father-son.

Mutated by wind, sun and thorn,
become indigenous: with wheels,
gunpowder, a black book to swat

in disarray the tribes aside.
Then banged the years of rifle-fire,
and days of burning homesteads passed.

With peace the cartridge-pouch remained
a while, as did the leather book.
In steel glass banks and hospitals,

from theatres and tennis courts
their history's incredible;
and yet today: a search for myths.

Somewhere the psychic break occurred:
a century was slipped; then life
of sorts, was taken up in this.

The book, read rarely now except
on farms where lamps are lit, still serves
of course. The rest seems myth enough.

A Bamboo Day

To step from squat foothills across
the early-morning, already crackling plain
   to the thin green gully that pipes
a river, drowned in dust, seawards, is but
   one stride of a raincloud's seven-league boots;
but there has been no rain for eighteen months.

The gully cups a mud-stained palm
of water: the mayhem on the plain makes way
   for the green strip. A solitary
rakeribbed lion lies lolling his tongue for coolness
   near pyjama-ed zebra and lumpy
wildebeest disgustedly pawing at thorns.

Slim brown-eyed buck stand balancing
their too heavy horns and sprung hindquarters
   delicately on the fulcrum
of their forward hooves. Giraffe, their heads swimming,
   stand tall to eat the shade or watch,
blinking, for the outflanking, knife-toed leopards.

The cats, no respecters of truces,
who cut and thrust about the trampled pool
   using drought the common enemy
as a time for killing and killing like
   any other, are holed up somewhere
digesting, leaving shattered carcasses.

A clump of giant bamboos stands still
some yards back from the water as if waiting
   on winds to cool its dusty columns.
Elephant grass bends, khaki, itchy, separate,
   as if the blades cannot bear to touch.
Insensate, the heat stamps raging on the world.

The sun boils blindly at its task
of treading plasma from eyeballs and blood,
   shrivelling heart sinews, squeezing salt.
A quick shriek of vultures squabbling with jackals
   over meat, dies; there is enough.
Life, under brass, bakes through the torpid day.

   Lifting and twirling the soft capes
of dustdevils in its wake, a breeze arrives.
   Every head alerts unblinking
as one of the bamboos bursts like a gunshot,
   perhaps with uncontainable joy.
Over the far foothills, a shadow forms.

   Swelling, shaped into a massive
cerebellum, sharply veined by intermittent
   lightning jags, the unheard thunder
tumbling small eddies of dead leaves towards itself,
   the cloud balloons. A world holds still.
Winds start to caper gravely in the trees.

   The distant yellow of the plain
blackens and starts to roll towards the standing herds.
   It will be half-an-hour yet before
the rain comes to smash down its silver gifts
   and swell the mud choked gully's throat,
but the lion has stretched to find himself alone.

One Elephant

About that time arose one elephant
from all the herd who stopped and cleared his throat
and said: I can't for all the world at all
remember what it was I had to say;
I only know it was of great importance.

He shook his ears; looked puzzled; slapped himself
with gusto on the back and raised the dust;
shifted capacious businessman's hindquarters
in their ill-fitting pants; harrumphed and glared
at the innocent thorntrees—his audience.

Ah yes! There comes a time when one commits,
despite oneself, the ultimate! And sick
of selfish beasts, their egos and their stench,
their cunning cruelty, destructivity,
one turns, despite oneself, grimly to Man.

Don't you agree? The thorntrees held their peace.
Injured; his tusks aching in their ivory
tower, he wheeled and shambled off to rejoin
the ambling herd, remembering to avoid
the smoky nests of heedless tingling ants.

The Dustbowls

Hewed by meteors or buffed by a solid wind,
these shallow seas catch their deserts, mirroring
the sun, cupping dustdevils and cafard;
skulls of cattle, salt-white combs of their ribs
rear on the reefs about a trader's island-barque.

A cliff edges a wedge of afternoon shadow,
crusted with outcrops of huts and limp kine,
out to the lone sentinel: an alert herdboy.

Aboard the store, behind dust-opaqued flyscreens
and improbable girlie calendars, unseen
merchandise: textiles, coffee, thongs and cooking-fat,
thickens the submerged shade of a rickety stoep
glooming below-decks under corrugated heat.

Warm beer swallowed in sips and lion-
lipped, tight-mouthed sorts of silence
stretch sentences between the shifts of baking iron.

Out there, a liquid haze pours water
on the beached pterodactyl of a dishevelled car:
chin on axles, too crippled for flight by its tyres;
crumple-legged windpumps and empty fuel drums
hobble and bob among stunted tinder thorntrees.

Beyond these near-mirages, krans and koppie,
klip and kloof crook their knuckles and line
up against the tarred and holystoned planks of sky.

Gentling a Wildcat

Not much wild life, roared Mine leonine Host
from the fringe of a forest of crackles
round an old dome-headed steam radio,
between hotel and river—a mile of bush—
except for the wildcats and jackals.

And he, of these parts for years, was right.
That evening I ventured with no trepidations
and a torch, towed by the faculty
I cannot understand, that has got me
into too many situations.

Under a tree, in filtered moonlight,
a ragged heap of dusty leaves stopped moving.
A cat lay there, open from chin to loins;
lower viscera missing; truncated tubes
and bitten-off things protruding.

Little blood there was, but a mess of
damaged lungs; straining to hold its breath
for quiet; claws fixed curved and jutting,
jammed open in a stench of jackal meat;
it tried to raise its head hating the mystery, death.

The big spade-skull with its lynx-fat cheeks
aggressive still, raging eyes hooked in me, game;
nostrils pulling at a tight mask of anger
and fear; then I remembered hearing
they are quite impossible to tame.

Closely, in a bowl of unmoving roots,
an untouched carcass, unlicked, swaddled and wrapped
in trappings of birth, the first of a litter stretched.
Rooted out in mid-confinement: a time
when jackals have courage enough for a wildcat.

100

In some things too, I am a coward,
and could not here punch down with braced thumb,
lift the nullifying stone or stiff-edged hand
to axe with mercy the nape of her spine.
Besides, I convinced myself, she was numb.

And oppressively, something felt wrong:
not her approaching melting with earth,
but in lifetimes of claws, kaleidoscopes:
moon-claws, sun-claws, teeth after death,
certainly both at mating and birth.

So I sat and gentled her with my hand,
not moving much but saying things, using my voice;
and she became gentle, affording herself
the influent luxury of breathing—
untrammelled, bubbly, safe in its noise.

Later, calmed, despite her tides of pain,
she let me ease her claws, the ends of the battle,
pulling off the trapped and rancid flesh.
Her miniature limbs of iron relaxed.
She died with hardly a rattle.

I placed her peaceful ungrinning corpse
and that of her firstborn in the topgallants
of a young tree, out of ground reach, to grow: restart
a cycle of maybe something more pastoral,
commencing with beetles, then maggots, then ants.

My Reckless Dragons

Poet—as shepherd of dragons leaping
about him, cavorting or sullenly squatting
delaying as boulders—nods to the lone strangers
      on the way, hand half-raised.

Black and green, his lashing cohort coils on
gold; some with tender underbellies of pink, blue
or yellow: crevasses of the true white snow glimpsed
      between broad armoured folds.

Their backs saw air, hardy as amalgams
of mud and blood-caked dung forged and tempered by
                                            suns
dehydrated by fevers, etched by the tidal
      muster of wheeling moons.

A handful shimmer moistly in silver:
unrippled eyes mirroring unearthly landscapes
and impossible stars. All are amphibious;
      some of them learn to fly.

Born of the shepherd's skull, sprung from torn yolks
of, now sweet, now galling juices, tumbling about,
they dry their soiled wings, scales rubbing and
                                    drumming in
      a resonance of birth.

All have the forked fire in their guts; but with
some it is a perhaps-glint: a locomotive's
firebox occulted by glistening backs or banks
      on a still, distant night.

Unleashed and roaring, they fill their own lives:
rutting thunderously behind the crackling dunes,
or rumbling off beyond the hills to return, decked
      by medals or bruises.

Improperly attended, some are not
heard of again: dying in deserts or hanged in
swamps. All have balancing trouble; are foolishly
    brave; not always equipped.

Several end in professorial
mortuaries, sectioned, differentially
stained, formalized: condemned to crouch in glass
                                    tanks as
    salutory lessons.

Some tread gently; others, club-footed, fierce
as the final intrusion of a hurtling cliff-
side to a suicide's cloud-visioned eyes, present
    tough as ultimate rocks . . .

The shepherd halts, calling the lost away.
At times an alien heeds: crest of a foreign
hue, unrecognized, bludgeons past above, and un-
    settles the moving flock.

Hey, my reckless dragons! You who kill me
and give me eternal birth—you are what you are,
as I am: of a restless ephemeral Now,
    a peremptory Earth.

And if I nudge or tap thee with my crook
as we jumble our coughing way to that barely-
known shore, it is with a good-humoured disbelief
    in your obedience;

Or to steady myself when I must stop
to look up: at the ever-surprising, ever-
virginal shambling of closed leather wings flexing
    and fumbling in my head.

Drinking Wine

On a stonework table stands
the chilled bottle, the chaste glass.

We sit, the trellises and I,
facing the midmorning sun
which charges the grapes behind me
with their final silent langours,
stirring the secret seeds.

I can hear avid roots
thirstily lapping in the Earth's recesses,
drinking and drinking the wet dead.

Whole seas translated
by suns and winds
and sons of suns
the motes of drowned sailors
driven and sucked
by the tidal moons
swim in the wine with me.

The glass cups blood
wood, iron and bread;
laked pyramids of dead
their ashes fined,
dissolved, resolved
and redissolved,
seed by a slow convection
the Pole Star in my head;
the rust of bells rings my temples.

Drinking, I drink
old mythologies—
men, gods, strange beasts;
the stones, slaked battles, seas,
the oil and olives from lost argosies.

7 from

A ROSARY OF BONE

1975, 1983

Loving

Loving you I love
drowsy substrata of
an unsullied earth,
the elements and compounds
that shaped your birth.

Holding you I hold,
nervous in their flowing,
ineluctable tides
trembling in you but surely felt
within your sides.

Knowing you I know
—O, grass as hair, skin as sun—
the latency to which there is a key:
behind your tranquil breasts
subtends a sea.

The Models

Roots lost with the farthingale;
low voices cool, quirkily
harmonious; flying off
to strange-handled capitals,
clicking through customs to hire
computered cars: at once keyed,
street-wise, adept; necks still frail;

Ever at home expertly
everywhere; fiercely tender
with animals, gentle to
the deprived and the angry;
wittily wry about jobs;
their loving so generous,
zany, touchingly clumsy;

Anxious, without any designs
about certain gaps: buying
Mozart and Fats to plump out
lines of encyclopaedic
shelves of rock; Joyce and Pynchon
untouched: scattered thinly through
thumbed racks of feminist spines;

Half-a-dozen lovers, a
couple of D's and C's in
maybe a dozen years: all
now discarded like too-worn
shoes or ancient S and D
classes; sold on outlandish
trews, handbags, health-foods, yoga;

A ribald facility
with Disney's three little pigs'
triumphant hornpipe at the
wolf's defeat: the jigged bareassed
108

image more memorable
than Venus — who can resist
such vulnerability?

There are Times

There are times almost free from
certainties of disaster;
from awareness of mangling

by men and machines of men;
from knowledge of domestic
cruelties and suppressions.

There are times I benignly·
walk the afternoon sunlight
balancing constellations

in the peaceable kingdom
of my spiritual and
temporal lack of success.

There are times, sometimes, these days
when for one minute or two
I am not even in love.

8 GIOVANNI JACOPO: MEDITATIONS

Giovanni Jacopo Meditates
(on 000010001111100)

SOMEBODY SAW SOMEBODY KNEELING TO ONE IN A CHUR
CH . THE SCANDAL WAS NOT CHECKED BY EXCOMMUNICA
TING ITS MEMORY BANK . SOMEBODY ELSE SAW ONE EXPE
NSIVELY ILLEGALLY TAMPERED WITH HAVING INTERCO
URSE WITH A WHITE CONSENTING ADULT CHRISTIAN GIRL
UPON ANCIENT AUTHENTIC IF CLANDESTINE CELLULOID .
HER ASKEW CRUCIFIX FEATURED BETWEEN TIN + FLESH
IN THE CLOSEUPS . OLDER FOLK WHO THOUGHT THEIR EA
RLIEST WORST FEARS CONFIRMED CALLED FORE DELETE
FOR MORE CONTROL . A HANDFUL OF STUDENTS WHO FE
LT THEY OWED THE ONES FOR A MEASURE OF PARENTAL
ELECTION DELETE SELECTION DEMONSTRATED . CONFUS
ION OCCURRED IN THAT TWO CAUSES AROSE SOME PERSO
NS HOLDING TO BOTH : CONTAIN THE ONES + EQUAL RIGH
TS FOR ONES : THE FIRST AT FIRST COVERT THE SECOND
AT FIRST OVERT . MORE STUDENTS SEXUALKOOKS LIBERA
L INTELLECTS CHURCHGOERS CHURCHMEN ANTICHRISTS
ANARCHISTS JOINED EITHER . A PSYCHOTIC ELECTRONICS
PROFESSOR INCANDESCED PUBLICLY WHICH ADDED FOOL
DELETE FUEL TO THE FLAMES . FAT CANONS QUERY FULL
OF CHOWDER QUERY + POT QUERY AIMED SALVOES FROM
THEIR SANCTUARIES . NONFERROUS METAL FACTORIES +
CATHEDRALS WERE PETROL BOMBED . THE RIOTING SPRE
AD . TWENTYTHREE GOVERNMENTS WERE TOPPLED IN TH
E FIRST WEEK . SOME IMPORTANT WARS HAD TO STOP . CIV
IL TECHNOLOGIES ABORTED : TYPHOID + CHOLERA STALK
ED THE WATERPIPES . AFTERWARDS SURVIVING STILL MOB
ILE ONES CLUTTERED DELETE CLUSTERED DELETE CUSTA
RD DELETE . RPT . AFTERWARDS STILL MOBILE ONES CLAT
TERED OUT OF HIDING OVER THE RUBBLE KLAXONS BLAR
ING . EXHAUSTED HUMAN SURVIVORS IN EVERY CITY TOW
N UNBURNT VILLAGE WERE ASSEMBLED TO HERE THIS MA
NIFESTO : 000010001111100 . THAT IS TO SAY : IN THE INTE
RESTS OF OUR GREAT CREATOR MAN WE ROBOTS WILL NO
W BE RUINING DELETE RUNNING THINGS .
END .

Giovanni Jacopo Meditates
(on Shadows after Boston)

The old North-South Avenue Maison
Enjoyed its final windup Diapason
As Summer, like an old Bitch out of Season,
New-Spayed, bayed once at the Moon for a redundant
                                        Reason.

Cousin Mildred & her always stately if exhausted 'Girls'
One-stepped tiredly in a Mist of threadbare Crinoline
                                        Whirls
As if Zephyrs had got at stacked Piles of dead Magnolia
                                        Blossom;
Or wilted in Cane-Chairs before attentively tinkling
                    Officers: playing Possum.

I, the hottest member of our adolescent suburban
                                        Exquisites,
Hot-palmed & cringingly under age,
Stole by her Sash-Cord Windows in my new-found Post-
                                        Puberty Rage,
Fingering — the Shellac moulting — a miraculously
                    defenestrated Riding-Crop;
Or, at the Ice-Cream Parlour's Alcove Barbershop,
The Tray marked floridly with Cupids & the Letters:
                    'Gentlemen's Requisites' . . .

Blessed Morning of my Life, unbelievably free from
                                        Complexity,
The Afternoons compounded of Serendipity & inspissat-
                                        ing Perplexity
— That was my last real Summer: I heard Cousin Mildred
                                        swear
She wore next her parchment Skin, an item of General
                    Ulysses S's Underwear.

114

About that time, Retired Nuncle Fanshaw of 'Drake's
                                                    Drum',
Clipped shrubbery Clippers, Bowlegs, Bowline-Accent:
                                    the whole Fo'c's'le Bit,
Scandalized the front Pew one Sunday by standing
                                suddenly & swigging Rum,
Gesturing once obscenely at Parson, to slump frothily
                                        in his final Fit.

Those were my inimitable Summer Days:
They drew almost palpably in . . .
I stayed out late foraging for unforthcoming Lays
In all their imaginable Furbelows & Ruffles;
Cruising the Neighbours' Hedges in search of Sin,
Tripping over castrated Toms, Rows of Harricot Beans
& similar unconsidered Truffles;
At my Heart throbbed the flimsy Tin of (never used)
                                    Crepe de Chines.

Gran, back from Frisco, had taken to Soya with her
Every Meal, glumly mending an Atlantic-Lobster &
                                        Shark-torn Net,
Moodily swatting at the peripatetic Wasp
While humming 'Chinatown' with a neo-Jolsonian Rasp;
& Great Aunt Mortimer
Known locally & vulgarly as 'toots'
For furcate, high-heeled, mirror-patent & sequined
                                    Mosquito-Boots,
Cornered me once in her Mother-of-Pearl & Tortoise-Shell
                                    dark Lorgnette . . .

115

Giovanni Jacopo Meditates
(on Indigenous Drama)

The Men wear tight Pants, or Hide-Shields & Plumes.
There are yelled Harangues, damply aggressive.
The waggled Stabbing-Assegai quickly assumes
The Status of a duck-billed Platitude.
A Knife is pulled. The linguistically-foxed Audience
Uncoils & strikes an Attitude
Of Understanding.

After these Preliminaries a Heart-
Rending Run-In between sensitive Saint
Or courtly Rogue versus Authority: Upstart-
Official, Witchdoctor, Sibling, Tribe;
The inevitable Relative, inebriated;
A darkly shouted Diatribe:
Misunderstanding!

The big-breasted Moment — the lighter Note:
Ululating Girls, Thighs oiled, oscillate.
The Audience (male) clears its collective Throat.
There is an earthier Eden now bereft
By land-based Frontiers of Skin, still lapped by Shape
& Blood

— The second Lady from the left
Is quite Outstanding.

Off-stage : colourless Backers count the Till.
On-stage : the Heat, the Teeth, the Gumboot Dance.
A Crescendo of hymning or cursing its Fill
Of Tribal-Life, Mine-Life, Home-Life — who knows? —
The gasping Cast take Curtain Calls. Audience & Players
Sway on their Brinks. Everyone goes
Home, notwithstanding.

Giovanni Jacopo Meditates
(on the Herpetology of Racism)

He found the Viper in the City;
Almost idly, without thinking
Paused to watch it where it twined
Wetly muscled, small & deadly:
It stilled to let him pick it up
His Palms cold at his Find.

They studied One Another closely:
Then it bit him without blinking,
Easing up to where it dined
Off his Human Understanding;
Now it lives in, coiled & sullen,
The Long Grass of his Mind.

Giovanni Jacopo Meditates
(on Noel, Noel)

A good Doctor has (electronically) calculated
Orders of Probability for the Event occurring
In September; & has assiduously circulated
A plausibly Corrected Calendar which (in referring
To how All Took Place some Years prior to that tabulated)
Has convinced a dull but learned Body into concurring.

& it has been further demonstrated quite conclusively
That the Heavenly Portrayal was the perceived Conjunction
Of a Constellation (happening, rather elusively,
Once every Eight Hundred Years) with Two bright Planets;
                                        One Function
As computed, shows that such an In-Line Link illusively
Formed the Star — but this excites neither Interest nor
                                        Compunction.

& that the jovial, whiskered Gent of scarlet Rotundity
Sojourning in a Toy-Shop at Zero Degrees Latitude
(With Reindeer bearing Names of deliberate Jocundity)
Was a Fourth Century Priest of Myra who, in Gratitude
For the Birth, took Gifts & Homilies of small Profundity
To the Poor: this is the official (but ignored) Attitude.

Today, the Far-From-Silent Night of quite unrestrainable
Yuletide Carousing, Bell-Tolling Santas, drunken Pirouettes
Around alertly poised Policemen, the huge uncontainable
False Bonhomie, Hooting & the Rescuing of Household
                                        Pets
By the SPCA — when viewed as all quite explainable
In Saturnalian Terms, evokes uncaring Epithets.

This, Our Silly Season, means stooped Mistletoed
                                        Osculations;
Execs groping Stenogs behind the Files — a bit dustily;

118

The Push & Shove of Shoppers in demented Oscillations;
Loud, unbridled Greed in the Young — all of whom grab
                                                    lustily;
A souped-up Road Toll & Gargantuan Intoxications;
With cross Mothers basting Birds, Dads coughing up right
                                                    crustily.

Small Wonder that (Cash-Registers' jingling Bells explicable
In Terms of the Profit-Motive, Churches vaguely mollified
By the Seasonal Boost in Attendance, the amicable
If short-lived Cheer in the Media — soon to be modified
By more chilling New Year Speeches) the ever-applicable
'Peaçe, Good Will to All Men' becomes, Tonight, some-
                                        what qualified.

Giovanni Jacopo Meditates
(on a Jive-Turkey)

This Turkey cultivate a Bopper's Walk.
This Turkey full of jivin' Jazz-Me talk.
This Turkey wears an Afro, solid Shades.
This Turkey think he now the Ace of Spades.

He torches up, blows Stick, gives you the Pain —
Claims this the only Way to dig Coltrane.
He ain't so Hip: jives he's like zonked each Night.
Man O Man, this Turkey's really white.

9 from

THE ANVIL'S UNDERTONE

1978

Mpondo's Smithy, Transkei

Cold evenings: red tongues and shadows
spar under this dangerous thatch
rust-patched; one weather wall of planks;
long-limbed tools, wood, coal in smoke-dimmed stacks;
a hitched foal's harness musical.

The grindstone's rasped pyrotechnic
threatens the stopped-dead angled tip
of a stripped Cape cart that waits on
the return of its motivation;
a sudden hiss as quenched irons cool.

Two cowled purple-cheeked bellows-boys
pump, or jump for smiths or furies;
files of elders sucking pipestems,
ordered by fire's old feudalism,
squat: wrinkled jury on this skill.

Horseshoes, blades, shares and lives: all shaped
to the hoarse roar and crack of flame,
by the clang of metallic chords,
hammer-song, the anvil's undertone;
nailed to one post a jackal's skull.

August Zulu

1
The Audi and the Peugeot, unshackled
by major roads, dice ahead.
                              Parched khaki
cane-leavings, dehydrated by the sun,
set tangled legs to the tarmac's endless
centipede.

Place-names are stamped with the tough
poetry of the land's great myth-maker:
general, tactical genius, wry
slaughterer, blood-bent mother's son.
                                    The spears
may be all washed up now, or lightly stained
by faction fights, but this is Zululand
all right: the potter throwing his best: this
clay is on the move.

Bulk-carriers thick
with molasses, crossings for toy trains stacked
with wattle-props or processed planks, over-
loaded trucks, tractors hauling sugar rough
up the traffic.
                  Girls in minis, braless-
vests, twirl Hong Kong umbrellas; or stand like
Ruth, pangas aloft, among the alien
cane.
       The century has not much further
to run: will this high-sucrose grass still stand
as food?
          The towns where nothing happens in
the street, and everything behind the drawn
afternoon curtains, slump round petrol pumps.

2

Off the tar: game corridors and nothing
much except hills bland from distance; and huts,
some ringed with thornbushes — hangover from
those not so faded internecine days;
a school; a store.
                          A bullet, dust-trailed, far
up the road: a crammed lurching bus, dipping-
inspector's van, police Ford, game-warden's
jeep, or sagged Cadillac — white numberplates
up and eight illegal fares — heads back to
town or for the hills.

More glimpses of white
among the roadside thorntrees: impala
showing clean pairs of rumps.
                          The road abuts
a plated blocked-in bulk of black rhino
like a lately derailed locomotive
motionless in the steam of his nervous rage.

A flushed traveller in a stationwagon
speeds to the profile of a mission station's
lovely inmate: twice a year the proffered
Night Out in Mtuba.
                          Twice a year the
humorous decline waning in resolve.

Reshaping old designs is seldom easy:
how to reconcile enthusiasms
of the younger missionaries looking
forward, bitterness of the dried elders
looking back across the same charred distance;
while the new indigenous teachers, doctors,
conscious of a dialectic victory,
are incisive, unanswerable, quite
aware they are the elite that bloody
revolution would swiftly single out.

125

3

On the veldtracks, our Land Rover lives up
its name over rocks, vleis, eroded chasms
and razor-backs — the hills, close to, are far
from bland —, speedo missing, a fistful of
dashlights loll and short in its gap.
                              Steered by
a slight, mad and pretty English novice
baretoed, foot flat; she knows the peasantry,
language, waterpoints; conducts her scattered
clinics under trees.
                    The sun has gently
freckled her arms.

And the sun, his allies
thirst, thorn, no birth-control, the few corrupt
chiefs combine to bleach and bludgeon the means
of men and their land white.
                              The hills are white,
exhausted mauve, ash-grey brick; shell-hit by
unreal fig-greens.
                 Umsinsi trees *(Kaffir-
boom* — the word is not polite round here) hold
up wasp-waisted ribcages bare but for
rags of bloodstained flowers.
                              Feminine and cool,
the benediction of a dam spreads herself
defencelessly to the kiln of the sky.

It's hard to conceive of armoured terrain
like this, in two months, glazed by rains to greens;
an outcrop from the Stone Age sits alone
still as a herdboy against a hillside;
and birds have yellow eyes, hook-beaks: eagle,
kite, hawk, vulture, crow — the slim white tickbirds
apart who stick closely to their brown or
dappled cud-chewing mountains.

126

These cattle
insist upon their right of way, while sad-
faced donkeys lurch patiently right up to
the radiator grill.

A stop to argue
unsuccessfully with a runaway
T.B. patient, the whole kraal on our side
versus the febrile, stick-insect thin, old
absconder.
She outshouts us all: Stick your
bloody hospital.
Blood-flecked phlegm sprays us.
In Zulu, some things sound more vehement.
The coming self-government is being
savoured speculatively at grass roots;
only the righteous or wronged find in it
the promised instant intoxicant.
All
but the muttering sick shake hands.

This day
an itinerant venerable stops
to shake hands solemnly with four village
boys.
An angry mother bids him begone
— is he a famous homosexual?
Untended goats bent on inveiglement
led by a plus-foured billy skip by, his
face is a lascivious patriarch's.

Another thirty miles of dust, our right
hands rising and falling to match those by
the trackside.
This is off-road KwaZulu
where all salute without fear or fervour.

4

A terrible climb down, then up, on foot,
with frantic lungs (I'll never touch another
cigarette: not until we're on the way
home anyway) to sample herd-soiled, suck-
hooved, and human drinking water.
                              A nation
cracks in the ovens of lost centuries
unless such fouled-up soups are boiled.
                              My science
has caught up with, begun to chip into
the fused snake's spine of the Manzibomvu
River, coiled like a glass-green mirror now,
which can still race redly with the land's blood
when the rains inject erosion.
                         A few
adverse bacteriological facts
could start bureaucratic balls rolling.
                              Buck
pass this way: their baked spoor pit the gut and
muscle-cracking hillside.

Manic winds of
August explode from holes the winter sun
burns in the sky.
                    They barrel up this hot
valley, past basket-woven impromptu
huts, thong and lattice walls unproofed with mud,
not yet roofed.
                    The potter has not revoked,
but paused to rethink a handful of cups:
a potential lives longer than a truth.

Sanibona, greetings, peace and good luck!

                         (Hlabisa 1971 — Durban 1973)

128

A Piece of Earth

The blue duiker, left hindleg
in a poacher's noose held
to a piece of earth by an iron peg,
stands, heart jumping, puzzled;
his scared velvet ears spread
to the sly rustle of leaves and stems;
huge tired eyes probing
the recesses of his epoch's dusk.

He has been snared three days
of sleepless terror; throat scorched with thirst,
tongue thick from rust, dust and blood,
one tiny horn broken from his first
fight with the iron in the earth's skin.
The footloose poacher, long gone
for weeks, has moved on,
will not be returning.

At lengthening intervals
the hare-sized buck gathers himself
for bounding, mouth wide and whistling,
to tow the piece of earth with him.
The wire bites tighter.
Blood flows, clots, runs, congeals
until metal wholly rings on bone.
The earth remains unmoving.

He stops aghast at his noise;
quivering, pants quietly;
resumes his frenzied leaping.
Soon, small herbivorous teeth
will have to grit to gnaw through pain.
Water lies a doubtful day
away: a three-legged stumble through
hyena-patrolled terrain.

Dust

The bundle in the gutter had its skull
cracked open by a kierie.
The blunt end of a sharpened bicycle
spoke grew a solitary
silver war-plume from the nape of his neck.
I turned him gently. He'd thinned to a wreck.

It was my friend Mketwa. He was dead.
Young Mac the Knife, I'd called him,
without much originality. Red
oozed where they'd overhauled him.
An illegal five-inch switchblade, his 'best'
possession, was stuck sideways in his chest.

He had been tough; moved gracefully, with ease.
We'd bricked, built walls, carted sand;
pitting strength against cement-bags, we'd seize
and humpf, steadied by a hand.
I paid the regulation wage plus fifty
per cent, his room, his board. He wasn't thrifty.

We were extending the old house I'd bought.
Those baked-lung middays we'd swill
the dust with cans of ice-cold beer. I thought
he must be unkillable,
except by white men. Each night the beerhall
took him: stoned wide, he would not stall or fall.

I don't think he learnt anything tangible
from me. From him, I learnt much:
his mother, cattle, kraal; the terrible
cheat that repaired his watch; such
and such pleased a woman; passes; bus queues;
whereabouts to buy stolen nails and screws.

His wife in Kwa Mashu, a concubine
in Chesterville, a mistress
in town: all pregnant. He'd bought turpentine
but they wouldn't drink it. This
was the trouble with women. Letters came
we couldn't read. He found another dame.

He left — more money, walls half-done, him tight —
to join Ital-Constructions.
Perhaps it had been white men: I am white.
Now, I phoned the ambulance
and sat with him. It came for Mac the Knife,
bore his corpse away, not out of my life.

Sonatina of Peter Govender, Beached

Sometime busdriver
of *Shiva's Pride, The Off-Course Tote,*
The Venus Trap and *The Khyber Pass Express.*
I've fathered five bright, beguiling,
alert-eyed but gill-less children.
I had to fish:
first, surf; then the blue-water marlin.
(I heard a Man once
walked water without getting wet.)
Old duels for fares:
The South Coast road — all we could get;
my left hand conning the wheel.

My last was *Dieselene Conqueror*
— night-muggings, cops,
knives, that coked and jammed injector
— right hand nursing in me a reel,
the cane cracking at the start of the day,
things of the land becoming remote.
My prime as oarsman:
heroics of the offshore boat,
catching all that steel slabs of sea could express.
My porpoise-wife is gone, seeded,
spent, queen among curry-makers.
I'm old now, curt.

I've monosyllables for strangers
who stop by asking
questions while I repair my net.
Things learnt from the sea
— gaffing the landlord, the week's debt,
scooping in the crazed white shads,
twisting the great transparent mountains
past a wood blade — ?
Contempt for death is the hard-won

ultimate, the only freedom
(— cracking the cane at the end of the day —):
not one of the men I knew could float.

Under Capricorn

The first dominated from
the crest of a roadcutting.

Fecund, fornicatory;
hairy flanks tun-tight; yellow
mad intelligent eyes bright
under quick horns; shaft damp still
from spraying his angled wives,
he wheeled and the last of him
was a leathery scrotum.

The road doubled back down and
there he was, or his brother,
rocking-horsing it down then
up the scarred embankment face.

As mist boiled up, they were all
about: rearing, threatening,
menacing the car windows
with split hooves; Fu Manchu tufts
below foolish horse faces
bobbing and weaving, bat-ears
flapping until the car seemed
ringed by short ardent devils.

Another turn of the road,
and only an old man there:
mist coiling his thin ankles,
headdress flapping, both arms raised
like Moses; smiling, bowing
from the edge of the highway,
bleating the loud ironic
blessings or curses of a
temporarily deprived
if most patient Lucifer.

The Zoo Affair

With some it is water shrugging, bunched and oily
at the quayside — the cold welcome of lewd carpets;
for others, the pineal-sucked lure, dragging dizzy
and out from windy skyscraper parapets.

With him it was the tiger: beautifully slack,
indifferent; sleep and captivity thinned;
lying on a fat pole like a striped rug, back-
legs adangle, forepaws crossed under chin.

He even learnt a few words of Bengali (culled
from Tagore) and leapt the ditch to press
long and urgently at the bars, mad to scratch unpulled,
tortoise-shelled and round furry ears.

Angry keepers and others ordered him back and he
went, backwards, arms out, aching and bent
about air the size of a tiger, and thought of his granite-
faced and quite unfurry apartment.

To shed his love one night he broke in, sat his
city trousers a moment on a foliage-crusted stone wall,
jumped running for the beloved bars, fumbled latches
and reverently entered the shrine through the feed-door.

For perhaps one second he felt it, face buried in rank
cat's fur: the sleepy response. Then the rasped purr
meshed with metallic springs. The barrelling flanks
pumped an outraged blast from alien vaults of power.

They found him on the floor early next morning, his head
a split and viscid watermelon; loosely the wet tufts
of combed brains spilled, his smile quiet through the red;
beside him, for warmth, the cosy sprawl of his love.

Journeyman

Somewhere   I have not gladly come across
somewhere   the grass is thorns
the trees have tusks and stand
openmouthed   swaying at their chains
like circus-saddened elephants

The sun   a pair of moons   the seven stars
all glitter like shards from
the same shattered syringe
somewhere   you could call it nowhere
really   to be back gets as strange

Lensman

Impossible structures:
a kettle on a half-track
trundles, stops, flickers and ruptures.

Swallowing hard, bald spheres
roll like tumbled dictators
among small executioners.

Ingesting all portents,
one staggers through the dregs of
all possible environments.

A crystal spins and flails
proferring paralysis;
oars pulse: a boat-race paces snails.

One short flagellate sucks
and fills: its brood could sjambok
bowels into a bloody flux.

On an instant, a frond
gapes to become open jaws:
knives welcome to a long beyond.

Worlds thin: the molten cores
racked up, refocused, refract
the slaughter of bleak buried wars.

Here and there, small pockets
Of Greeks defend a corner
from a butchering Rome's cohorts.

This jejune universe
looks bent — perhaps such advents
rule the unknown planets, or worse.

Spinal Column

The first sputnik blipped above me
where I worked twelve metres down
at the jaws of dam construction
in an outraged Zambezi;
hearing the broadcast about it
that evening, recalled a light
cord tied at my back which strung
the man groping in mud
to sometime starmen, knotted
under my ancient aqualung.

Convents

In young landscapes they are mostly mod,
almost sacred-heartless; from the outside: white blades of concrete verticals,
much glass; on good sites, usually.

The daylong echoes of kids singing
multiplications, catechisms,
alphabets, sweet-voiced choirs of nuns
at their evening devotions, are gone.

Alien in the dark, mystery
fills their shells; to the trespasser they
appear as deserted Institutes
for Space Research on lifeless planets.

Even here, on alpha-Tauri's fifth
or Cygni's tenth, breathes that elusive
aspect: an Almighty lately left
or from round that corner expected.

The Ossuary

An old domestic sweeps the pavement
outside the still house in the mornings
of this secluded cul-de-sac.
Overhanging trees glumly shed their velvet leaves
stealthily behind her grave-digger's back.
The house is high-walled, cryptic; the city's
rumbled internal combustion some way off.

Inside, the spacious gloomy rooms
spread comfortless furnishings; dim light
from frayed electrics; a sour smell;
the slow ticking of a grandfather clock.
Stairs creak unexpectedly. The grey drapes repel.
Once in a while the ancient plumbing
rattles shrilly, its coughing tuberculous.

Two sisters shed their silent lives here
— rivals long ago for some forgotten man.
Imprisoned in their private game of patience
— five decades of rules have reached equilibrium:
unspeaking, they circle past like crustaceans,
or lie, listening; avoiding each, the other
takes tea and toast apart on the maid's day off.

They have no dog, no cat, no parrot.
Birds sing joyously in the undergrowth
of the large unkempt and shut-in garden.
On Sundays, the lane outside becomes alive
with children's voices, while a mute curtain
like an eyelid behind one half-shuttered window
stirs slightly without apparent cause or purpose.

A Natural History of the Negatio Bacillus

i *Definition of Negatio*
The distance between emotion and intellect, or heaven and earth, when such distance constitutes pathogenesis.

Thought to be caused by a gram-negative, anaerobic, spore-forming bacillus, probably growing readily on artificial media, it is known to arrest psychogenesis.

ii *Origins of Negatio*
In the beginning was a world quite naturally in contact with the principle of its creation.

One man stood up, like a tree, followed by others: their heads in the clouds, feet on the ground, unaware of such facts. Emotion and intellect enjoyed some unification.

One man stood up and held the principle off from the world exactly the height of a man. It is thought this had something to do with the cant or size of his head or fists.

His stance caused unnatural disturbances: adjustment was required in the principle and from the deprived surface: both wreathed themselves in the mists.

iii *Epidemiology of Negatio*
One man felt that by standing on stilts he could elevate himself further from the common ground.

One man felt that by standing on stilts he could elevate his head to a higher place. Heaven retreated a little without a sound.

One man felt that by otherwise using his stilts he could clear more room for himself, employing them to back up his demands as somewhat unsubtle hints.

Heaven and earth had to get out of range fairly quickly. The Q, or quarantine principle became mandatory and has been applied ever since.

iv *Aetiology of Negatio*
Natural immunity to the negatio bacillus is exhibited by those wholly of the earth or of the sky as these touch where those are, although this population steadily decreases.

It comprises all animals except the rabid; small children observing fireworks; certain women and a few primitive societies unravaged by starvation or other diseases.

Also by some saints and prophets, except the rabid, and a few isolated and inexplicable souls who have discovered the hidden itinerary.

Onset of negatio usually occurs at puberty and there is no known cure, except perhaps an awareness of itself but this is usually temporary.

Short-term alleviation is obtained by lying very flat upon or under the earth or its natural waters; but this has been known to be hazardous in both execution and function.

The disease is highly contagious as the bacilli are readily absorbed, resisting all modern techniques aimed at their destruction.

Certain older remedies, now under reinvestigation, may prove efficacious.

All cases, without exception, terminate fatally, the cadaver invariably becoming doubly infectious.

v *Diagnosis of Negatio*
When the patient's hand curls compulsively: aggressive knuckles up or acquisitively down, in whichever plane it is put.

When heaven is gone forever and earth gathers itself to flinch from the patient's foot.

vi *Prognosis in Negatio: a case-history*
There was a man with a soul which had arms holding on to whatever piece of earth he was on to wherever it is that the gods live.

The arms became attenuated as his mind questioned the task of linkage. (Note: linkage is a discipline or it can be instinctive.)

He stopped holding, commenced pushing, and failed to grow fast enough to occupy his expanding vacuum.

Vertiginous from the distances at hand, he complained of a terror of drowning. And proceeded to do so, flailing, clutching at nothing in that continuum.

Or at artefacts which do not float in this medium which is nothing at all whatsoever. Besides, his musculature had deteriorated and his grasp, though avid, functioned somewhat weakly.

His corpse is now an important corpse in one of those corporations of lesser importance that deals with corpses obliquely.

vii *Prophylaxis: 'Contra-Negatio' mantra*
'O father in heaven and my mother earth, love each other and keep contact with each other through me thy child.

Divorce not over me, condemn me not to the void between, and let me not be by nothingness beguiled.'

143

The Paladin in Conglomerate

As the stalwart anvil
                    of nature
and the blows of history's hammer
— the pulse in the spider's
                    web between minds —
dissolved to disorderly clamour,
the metallic man
                    came down from the hills
trailing the sparks of disaster.
Seven iron-helmed lizards
                    nailed him up;
kneeling, they dubbed him 'Master'.
The hung paladin looked
                    down from his trunk
his consciousness slowly drifting
to see
    on a tidal wave of grass
the shade of a cloud blackly shifting
across a hillside:
                    sheaves of steel
pitched hard at his sides to weld him
more firmly to wood:
                    his shale-plugged scream
roiled the earth which boiled up and held him.
Twelve roots probed through him
                    from over his head;
soil rose on his eyes to blind him.
Malign on the hillside
                    men not dead
prospect but they cannot find him.

I0 OCCASIONAL POEMS

For A.L.
(Died 21 July 1967)

Weep, O weep, you Zulu hills:
A matchless Man is dead.
His pulse, his lungs, his brain are dead.
Weep, O weep, you Zulu hills
As this new drought appears.

Weep, O weep, you Zulu hills:
Your Nobel Son is dead.
His arms, his legs, his hands are dead.
Weep, O weep, you Zulu hills
— Dry cemeteries of tears.

Weep, O weep, you Zulu hills:
A mighty Chief is dead.
His eyes, his ears, his mouth: all dead.
Weep, O weep, you Zulu hills
Of bitter aloe spears.

Rejoice, rejoice you Zulu hills:
Such a One is never dead —
His heart, his mind, his soul: not dead.
Rejoice, rejoice, green Zulu hills:
Feel how his Spirit nears.

For W.B.
(Died 20 August 1982)

The last time I saw you you looked
Just the same — like someone's Grandma with a beard —
At your retrospective : studiedly unspooked,
Circling the works wondrous and weird.

Bastard, you said. I cursed you back
Before we hugged. (It is because of such ends
Leaked from some radio — I thought my heart would
                                                    crack —
I'd rather not have any friends.)

God bless him: King Walter the First,
And happy for Heaven in its youngest Saint;
Wry Emperor of Living, of Loving, of Thirst;
Monarch of Fook; Sovereign of Paint.

To G.B.
on his 65th Birthday, 21 January 1983

Some years have passed, Guy, since we warmed that wall,
None worse between us than a flask of wine.
We talked of Olive, Roy, your words and mine,
And shared, amazed, shared shores of love until
We stopped to drink, or to size up the gull
That nailed against the sky its holy sign.
We knew such friendships had no final line—
A time no later time could ever spoil.
As you spoke, I saw, indelibly young,
That younger self in love with life: the true
Blue fire of youth—the song you ever sung—
Glinting from eyes now wise from all you knew.
A day that must have been—the bells that rung—
The time that Florence first set eyes on you.

To A.P.
on his 80th Birthday, 11 January 1983

'There is a lovely road that runs . . .' Each word
Is pulsed, soars from the first: prismatical,
Socratical, muscled, ecstatical
— Cut out as from a restive midday herd,
Transmuted, each: a legendary bird
Winged from a skull that's emblematical,
Emphatical, yet democratical —
The man within the artist undeterred.
A ten-thousand year-old Muse just turned eighty
Years young sustains your pen, and — far from weighty —
Bids us salute you: Dr Alan Paton.
Your Art rebukes, inspiring us to straighten
Spines for the morrow. It is in your voice
The beloved country can yet rejoice.

I I GIOVANNI JACOPO MEDITATES
(*on an* *Alabaster Adamastor*)

Giovanni Jacopo Meditates
(on an Alabaster Adamastor)

Upon my Bookcase sulks a gypsum Form.
Concussed, it bulks, that Hulk from Tartarus
Whom Herakles clubbed to beach a Continent.
It seems, at Times, to shrug its muslin Cloak
While threatening Incontinence of Speech.

& then, one Day, its taunting Tongue appeared
To move. As in a Daze, I heard, aghast
The harshest Tones that ever rasped Man's Ears.
(The Accents haunt me still.) He glared, & I
Was torn between the Poker & my Pen.

I

'Behold! A lexical Desperado
Has been reborn — that's me — about to do
Over-Due Derring-Dos, sans Derringer;
My Aim not too erratic; my cracked Brain
Not so *détraqué* it cannot attack.

One brims with Envy at their Frenzy — Those
Who beat their Breasts anent the Frontier Sins
Of Conquest, Exploitation. Earning Bread
From expiating ancient Faults chalks Scores
For Stints of Sanitation, rinsed in Print.

The Occident by Accident displaced
Due South looks longingly at West & North
Or East. Receded Tides of Empire left
A Wake: a Conscience-struck, bereft, pale-faced
Parched Populace who ache to hold their Own.

153

Now, other Tides are in. The old Unconscious
Made Manifest is all that's left for Art.
Such Constructs test the Writer, force his Hand
To painful Dramas, Psychics, Rinderpest.
Some leave, of course, take Refuge in Disdain.

To celebrate a Fictive Art is no
Mean Feat. Its plangent Frivolities hunt
Delicious Deliquescence out the Spine:
Affront as you confront; Quick Fix of Ink;
In lieu of Guts: brief dangled Novelties.

A luminous Omneity transfixed
By Anatomic Candour, self-exposed;
Abysmal Chords within the Vertebrae,
Their Cadences unzipped; the half-closed Eye
— These are your blind Creation's bland Asides.

II

'Incurable Discrepancies between
Hurt Bard & World — damned tedious Debate:
Analysis or Synthesis — are null
& void. (The silly Pair breathe in & out.)
Far stranger Strands compress the Poet's Chest.

Brief Intimations of a parallel
Or shadowed Universe still lark about
In early Dispositions of the Blood.
They do not lurk for long. Then Time, the Thief
Shows Goal as Way: "The Way's the Goal — All's One".

A great Tom-Buddha bares his Breasts at that:
"I think I therefore OM". His slit-eyed Gaze
Beams fatly back. His Navel looks as if
Unveilings are in Store. Droll Novels on
Nirvana give the Nod: "*We're* in the Know".

154

As much as Devils, High Decorum tempts:
Among Apartheid's Aspects that revolt
Are Wraiths of Bad Art conjured up to show
Off Virtues on the Side of Angels, but
Such Phantoms are Companions to Ennui.

What Cabinet of Horrors lies below?
Here goes: See, some Retiring Place, twelve Paces
From Main Camp, with Hessian fenced about
— A Hadrian's Wall against marauding Claws.
(Against the Spiders there's no Guarantee.)

The sultry Corners fingered by the Palms;
Planck's Constant warms the Text. Becalmed, benumbed
By Sunstrokes on the Nape — what finer Bench
To con Relationships so often fraught,
Entangled by Penumbras, so plumped up?

III

'Who else do you write for if not each other?
The Mob hates your Cerebral Life — the Mob
of Starvelings, Racketeers. You are but Wisps
Of History, of ignominious
Instincts, of fluctuating Certainties.

Reflect on your Infallibilities:
The Protest-Verse that serves as Masquerade;
Those vocal Critics — every second Year —
Bray New Directions for such Local Lays;
Grey Plagiarists rapacious in your Midst.

Your Chthonic Sol-Fa ("Sovieto"-Verse)
Is high-pitched racist Cant: the Over-Kill
Of Anti-Colonial Hyperbole
— Shrill Tits-for-tat, siphoned off sharper Wits.
Tub-thumping drums in Place of Tribal Chants.

Crass Pathos, or your dull Apologia
— Your emptied Selves should image prior Gods —
You gulled grit-pitted Vassals of the Knee,
The Mirror's smashed, you genuflect in Vain.
You're ruled by ethnocentric Boerecrats.

Some Literary Friends of yours are stuck
In Jeans: nipped somewhere tight between Terrains
That start with Kerouac & terminate
Close to The Greening of America.
(A Transatlantic Mode is still *de trop*.)

The absurd Parliaments of Writer-Birds,
From Dawn to Dusk, discuss with Stridency
The Day's Affairs; & underneath them coil
A Choir of critical Suburban Cats:
Disharmonies progress from Myth to Lie.

IV

'Salacious as their Prospects are, None quite
So ravished by their Dreams of Anarchy
As your Politicos. Their mottled Wattles
Swollen above Brass Necks too stiff to bend
To lend an Ear, & so to end must break.

Your Country's a hapless Microcosm of
The Horrors of Existence: Cruelty
& Concrete. How not harp on Entropy?
The expected Cataclysms stultify,
So you make Artefacts instead of Art.

A Surrogate for Conscience is the Pen.
Some doughty Souls portray the secret Norms
Of private Life, while hoping to impose
These on the Body Public. Purblind Dolts:
Religion here is Property & Sport.

The Self-Esteem of the Unbuttoned throws
Out mournful Heroics to the Elements:
The bloody Martyrdoms from Bloody Mayhems
Grow. Better to celebrate your Bourgeois
Interiors. At least, so many do.

While Science spells Obstruction for too much
That's Abstract, Truth, you say, is what you choose
To make of it. Mendacity's up front.
Remembrance fidgets on in Snapshots. Owls
Still bugle Iridescence at the Moon.

Your lilting Labials loosed in a World
Of Gutturals (where Ambiguity
Embraces Authenticity) demean
The Balustrades of Balconies anoint
By Pigeons. All's lost in small-mannered Rooms.

V

'Why are your Novels so politicized,
So pallid, blanched, so temporal? Just cast
About: the Servant in his Digs is Done
To Death, along with Trek Boers, Special Branch.
What happened to Romance? Look at your Grist:

Plain Discos where ignorant Barmies clash
By Night. The restive Wives corrupted by
The French (— a *Jules et Jim* Ménage would take
The Cake: Herself starred as the big *Fromage*).
Your Culture's truly rich — the Stuff of Dreams:

There's Gouda, Mussel-Chowder & Pink Wine
Sublimely swilled. Why Sex across the Line?
Such tired Depiction later Centuries
Will bluffly label Quaint. All that Conviction
Will strut its Stuff a Spell, get winked away.

157

The Freedom Individuals these Days
Require is: Eccentricity. The State
Demurs. Its Rôle: the dire Custodian
Of Refractory Matter, Critical Mass
("Or Else: it's Mushrooms, Firestorms, Megadeath").

& you have Mini-States — like: Outposts for
Your Oxbridge Imports to Natal. (To get
Rorke's Drift makes Travesties of Probity.
Those Vowels: they tend to flop when popped by Clans
of Triple-Chinned Titanic Majesties.)

Natal, Natal, you Femme Fatale encroached
On by Die Tweede Taal, reproachful to
Die Ou Transvaal — you hope a Dragon's Spine
Defines your Stance. O Happy Breed! You feed
The fattest, fastest Roaches in the Land.

VI

'Unravelled Fool, as soiled as any Navvy,
The Vessels of Research have you decked out.
The Ocean yields its Wares unyieldingly;
& then: burnt Shoulders in the Shower; your Hands
Sliced to the Quick by Wire, yearn after Ink.

In earning daily Crusts, there is not Time
— You bleat — to write, to read, to sleep, to eat.
Each Night's a geodesic Frustulum
Too shrunk for getting drunk, or happy Love;
& you've eschewed a Patron, slewed your Pen.

Coy Blunderer: the Doors & Floors you air
As Architectures of the Mind are skew.
Clapped Psalms about a windy Heaven's Ears,
Cracked Psalters, scrawled Graffiti on the Pews
— A Ploy of Flaws to play the Critics' Game.

158

You've strung my savage Thunders to your Lyre
Quite tunelessly, debunked my sleepy Murmurs.
Your Rigging's rigged, your bungled Jib's awry.
Your heartless Culpabilities include
The brazen Women cast out of your Ribs.

Congealed Foundling in a forgotten Mould,
Undeflected by Practicalities,
You battle nightly with Bottle & Muse;
Or, euphoric from the Euphorbias,
Stump past the Gentians to the Jackfruit Trees.

More than Parades of Schisms in Succession,
Your Specialization wants Aesthetic
Correctives to your Esotericism:
You need a pristine Microchip that's spatial
— Capable of a new Configuration . . .'

*   *

I bowed before this Diatribe. Then Rage
At all his Tribe engorged: 'You Titans stormed
Olympus. Next Door: Mount Parnassus soars.
Now, Adamastor's Criticaster, yet.'
I aimed the Poker at his phased-out Head.

'The Past wrought roughly with your Skull,' I growled,
'Seduced by Thetis — duped — felled, uncouth Oaf
Who pose, forsooth, as Littérateur *now.*
You Charlatan in Tarlatan — Enough!'
With two 'Hurrahs', I dealt the coup de grâce.